Hampton's
OLDE WYTHE

Hampton's
OLDE WYTHE

JEWEL OF THE VIRGINIA TIDEWATER

The Olde Wythe Neighborhood Association

Charleston · London

THE
History
PRESS

Published by The History Press
Charleston, SC 29403
www.historypress.net

First published 2014

Manufactured in the United States

ISBN 978.1.62619.265.2

Library of Congress CIP data applied for.

CONTENTS

FOREWORD

Olde Wythe is an eclectic assembly of tree-lined streets and houses, punctuated by a few shops and businesses, situated along the shore of Hampton Roads Harbor. Today, it is bounded by Hampton Roads, Pear Avenue (the border with Newport News), Kecoughtan Road and LaSalle Avenue. It is a large neighborhood composed of many smaller ones.

Indians lived for thousands of years alongside these coastal waterways. Today, place names such as Indian River Park and street names such as Kecoughtan Road, Pochin Place, Powhatan Parkway, Algonquin Road and O'Canoe Place located in the heart of Olde Wythe and near the shopping district first called Wythe are ever-present reminders of their existence. The English built here in the earliest days of settlement. It was largely a farming area at the beginning, dominated by the huge plantation along Hampton Roads called Celey. During the War of 1812, 2,500 British troops landed near Indian River Creek and marched on Hampton. Urban development did not blossom here until the late nineteenth century. George Wythe, elemental to the formation of an independent American democracy, lived a few miles away, and the name of Hampton's most important citizen was given to the area quite early.

When the Civil War came, the epic Battle of Hampton Roads, a naval battle between the *Monitor* and the *Virginia* (formerly the *Merrimack*), was fought just offshore. After the war, Wythe resident Captain J.C. Robinson, along with many others, made a living harvesting fish and shellfish, so working boats in the harbor and great piles of oyster shells on the shore were common local sights contributing to Hampton's reputation as "Crabtown." Developmental entrepreneur James S. Darling built a trolley line from Newport News that followed a direct route inland from the shipyard across intervening farmland to Hampton and Phoebus, allowing workers from sturdy working-class homes in the Wythe area to commute to the shipyard. The clang of streetcars meant mobility and a better income for locals and greatly increased the urbanization of the Wythe area. The varied and distinctive building styles of Wythe's homes reflect the evolution of the nation's vernacular architecture.

The Olde Wythe Neighborhood Association collaborated in the making of *Hampton's Olde Wythe*, published by Arcadia in 2006, an exceptional pictorial journey through the area's growth into the neighborhood that thrives today. Vigorous inquiry turned up useful photographs and much material that had been locked away for a good while and kindled curiosity about the region's bygone times. Heartened by the overwhelming reception to the first book, and possessing much relevant documentation and many stories from Wythe's historical legacy, the association determined to undertake a comprehensive interpretation of Olde Wythe, inviting various authors to help. The result is this volume, *Hampton's Olde Wythe: Jewel of the Virginia Tidewater*.

These well-crafted pages provide an insightful and important analysis of a distinct section of the city of Hampton. Reliable neighborhood histories are indispensable for a full understanding of the complex and problematic events making up Hampton's existence. Several other respected studies of aspects of Hampton's past have emerged in recent years. The Olde Wythe Neighborhood Association's work is an admirable addition, foregrounding the voices and stories of men, women and children who grew up in or contributed to Olde Wythe.

J. Michael Cobb
Curator, Hampton History Museum

Acknowledgements

Bethany Austin (Hampton History Museum)
Paul Emigholz
Carolyn Hawkins
Ed Hicks (Hampton History Museum)
Claudia Jew (Mariners' Museum)
Anne McHenry
Thomas Moore (Mariners' Museum Library)
Helen Sampson
Bill Sasser
Kelly Siegel

For additional information concerning the rich history of Olde Wythe,
visit www.oldewythehistory.com.

INTRODUCTION

As part of our twentieth anniversary commemoration of the Olde Wythe Neighborhood Association (OWNA), the OWNA is pleased to present this book as a sequel to *Hampton's Olde Wythe*, a pictorial history that was first published in 2006. This present publication contains newly researched material, much of which is published here for the first time, and permits the authors to provide to readers the results of their in-depth research. It brings to light many previously unknown historical vignettes of the Olde Wythe community of Hampton, Virginia, and weaves an intriguing and fascinating story of a community that is steeped in history.

Olde Wythe as we know it today is a vibrant community of approximately 1,500 households situated on the Lower Peninsula between the Chesapeake Bay and the James and York Rivers. Its boundaries include Kecoughtan Road to the north, La Salle Avenue to the east, Pear Avenue to the west and the historic waterway of Hampton Roads to the south. This waterway has played an amazingly important part in the history of the United States over the past five hundred years. As befits its rich history, the community is named after one of Virginia's most respected but little-known signers of the Declaration of Independence, George Wythe.

The State of Virginia and City of Hampton have recognized the rich historical significance of this area by erecting over a dozen historical markers in Olde Wythe to commemorate the many events of historical significance that have occurred in or near this community. There are six waterside vista points overlooking Hampton Roads along Olde Wythe's main thoroughfare, Chesapeake Avenue, with benches where visitors can read these markers and observe oceangoing merchant cargo vessels; across Hampton Roads to the south, they can view the unique operations of the world's largest naval base.

Chapters in this historical book further refine the history of Olde Wythe by taking the reader from the first Native American settlement established here through the English exploration and the first commercial development of its shores. Additionally, the impact of military operations is detailed from the British landing in 1813 and subsequent burning of Hampton through the Civil War to the passing of Major General Patton's task force off its shores en route to the 1942 Allied invasion of North Africa. For the first time, the history of Olde Wythe's growth and development, as well as its social, educational and cultural heritage, is accurately documented, as is the background that describes the leaders who made such a positive impact in guiding Olde Wythe's future. Additional chapters recount the excavation of Native American artifacts here in the 1950s; the growth of the 1890s Hampton Roads Golf and Country Club, which hosted President Wilson; the history of Wythe's schools; and the discovery and documentation of Olde Wythe's "kit" homes.

The Olde Wythe Neighborhood Association greatly appreciates the dedication of the authors, who diligently researched and wrote each chapter. Additionally, extensive credit must also be given to those named in the acknowledgements who labored for many long hours to ensure the accuracy and continuity of this book. The association hopes that this book will serve as a foundation from which future generations will discover the rich past of both Olde Wythe and Hampton, Virginia.

Olde Wythe Neighborhood Association
July 12, 2014

Chapter 1

How We Became Olde Wythe

In 1634, Elizabeth River Shire was the name given to land in the southeastern part of Virginia by order of the king of England. The land included Wythe and extended across the harbor into Norfolk and beyond. In 1636, this land was divided, and the land north of the harbor was called Elizabeth City Shire. A short time later, this same land was renamed Elizabeth City County, often abbreviated as ECC. Later, when the county was divided into three districts, one was called the Wythe Magisterial District in honor of George Wythe, a native of Elizabeth City County, whose house was located within the boundary of the Wythe District. George Wythe was a signer the Declaration of Independence as well as a noted teacher of law at the College of William and Mary. The Wythe District grew as a suburb of the cities of Hampton and Newport News, attracting executives and blue-collar workers from Newport News Shipbuilding as well as employees of the many government installations in the area, including Langley Field (U.S. Army Signal Corps) and the National Advisory Committee for Aeronautics. As the area job market grew, so, too, did Wythe.

The Wythe District was the largest and most populated in the county. The boundary lines of Wythe began at Salters Creek, which today is part of the city of Newport News; extended to the York County line; and then went east to the southern branch of the Back River and, finally, south to the Hampton Roads Harbor, going around the city of Hampton and linking up with Sunset Creek.

The current name, the Olde Wythe, did not exist until 1995. Before that time, the area was Wythe Neighborhood, and prior to that, this part of the city was simply called Wythe.

Hampton's Wythe District. *Library of Congress.*

The Wythe "name game" began in 1992, when the city of Hampton embarked on a new neighborhood initiative. The program was designed to organize neighborhoods throughout the city, giving them boundaries and a name and allowing each to have a voice at city hall on behalf of the people living within the designated areas. The city was divided into ten districts, each with a district volunteer commissioner, whose job was to work with civic associations within his or her district. One of the districts was called Greater

Wythe, with boundaries at West Pembroke Avenue and Queen Street to the north, LaSalle Avenue to the east, Hampton Roads to the south and the Hampton/Newport News city line and Aberdeen Road to the west.

Over two dozen civic-minded residents from Wythe volunteered to determine a plan for the Greater Wythe District. The group established subcommittees to meet with residents as well as business and church leaders to seek information in order to determine if or how Greater Wythe would be divided into smaller neighborhood/civic groups. After meeting once a month for nearly a year, the group decided to establish boundaries within the Greater Wythe District so that smaller civic associations could be formed instead of having one large association representing all of Wythe. Boundary lines were drawn, and the members of the committee then went back to their respective areas to organize civic/neighborhood associations. These areas included LaSalle Acres, Wythe-Phenix, Park Place, Rosealee Gardens and Olde Wythe. Other areas of the Greater Wythe District were not organized at this time, as there were no representative volunteers involved in the planning meetings.

With boundaries of Kecoughtan Road, Hampton Roads Harbor, Hanover Street and Pear Avenue, the Wythe Neighborhood Association was established. A board of directors was assembled, and bylaws were written. The first board members knew that it would be hard to engage all residents with an executive board of directors of just five members. They wanted to make sure everyone in the neighborhood felt as though he or she had a voice on the board and therefore created district representative positions as voting members of the board. To implement this, the Wythe neighborhood was divided into nine districts, thus giving each subdivision equal voting representation. The board wanted to have a neighborhood association for the entire neighborhood, not just parts of it. It was decided that the representative would have to live within that district and would be responsible for bringing concerns of their neighbors to the board for action. The officers of the board could live anywhere within the established boundaries of the Wythe neighborhood. With the addition of the district representatives, the fourteen-member Wythe Neighborhood Association Board of Directors was established.

In 1998, the Wythe Neighborhood Association Board of Directors began discussing a name change for the area. They proposed adding the word "Olde" to the name of the neighborhood. The board wanted to set this part of the Wythe District apart from others that were also using the name "Wythe." In an article in the 1999 winter issue of the Wythe Neighborhood Association's newsletter, the board announced that the vote on the name change would be held at the spring membership meeting. The article stated, "For years realtors, businesses, and even the City has been using the name Wythe to describe locations outside of the boundaries of the neighborhood we have known for decades as Wythe…it is common to look at homes for sale in magazines and see properties that are in poor condition and priced well below median price of homes in our neighborhood. This gives an incorrect impression to folks moving into our area…it will also allow realtors and businesses to trade off our good location, reputation, charming properties and high values."

After a coordinated effort between the city of Hampton and the volunteers of the Olde Wythe Neighborhood Association, in September 2008, the neighborhood was placed on the Virginia Landmarks Registry. At the time, with over two thousand contributing buildings used to determine eligibility, Olde Wythe was the largest area in the Commonwealth of Virginia to be given this designation. In October 2011, after again working in conjunction with the city of Hampton, Olde Wythe was placed on the National Register of Historic Places. This honor recognizes the historic value of the neighborhood and its contribution to the growth of Hampton and Newport News. With both of these recognitions, Olde Wythe is one of the most desirable historic places to live or visit on the Peninsula.

But what history surrounds the growth of Olde Wythe into today's vibrant community of over 1,400 households? Normally, developers purchase land, select a name for their new neighborhood, lay out streets, build homes, sell the homes and then leave. Most of these types of neighborhoods have homes that are similar in size and shape and are even painted alike. Many lack the charm and character of older neighborhoods.

Prior to the Civil War, there were few houses built in the area now referred to as Olde Wythe. After the war, between the 1880s and the 1890s, northerners relocated to the area and bought land cheaply, primarily through foreclosures and back taxes. The first homes were built along the Hampton Roads Harbor, taking advantage of the summer breezes to keep cool and the use of the waterway for business and relaxation. It wasn't until late in the 1890s that home lots were first offered for sale on the west end of the neighborhood on land that was once called Celey Plantation. Celey Plantation was named after Thomas Celey, who, in 1624, bought the land on the north side of today's Salters Creek in the city of Newport News (at the time a part of Elizabeth City County's Wythe District) from Robert Saltford, who had patented the land in 1611 from the Virginia Company of London and built a tidal mill. At the time Celey bought the land, the creek was called Saltford Creek.

Celey Plantation started with five hundred acres and became the largest plantation on the Peninsula, eventually growing to over two thousand acres. Over the course of the plantation's life, the acreage changed, but the plantation house and the property closest to the harbor remained in the hands of Thomas Celey's family. Built in 1705 by Colonel William Wilson, who had become owner of the plantation through marriage, a plantation house sat facing the Hampton Roads Harbor in the area of today's Riverside Rehabilitation Center. The brick plantation house was two stories high with a columned portico and two single-story wings at each end. The house stood among elm trees overlooking landscaped terraces that were planted with colorful shrubs and flowers and led to the water's edge. Colonel Wilson moved into his home in 1706 and started raising crops for the growing population of the area. He also used the port in the town of Hampton to sell his crops elsewhere.

Celey Plantation became a footnote in the history of the United States when a young man named George Washington came to the plantation to visit Sally Cary, one of the daughters of Colonel Miles Cary, who had later acquired the plantation through marriage. Colonel Cary was a surveyor, a justice of the peace and the collector of duty in Elizabeth City County.

Washington, who was just sixteen years old at the time, had first met Sally in Williamsburg and was immediately smitten with her beauty and grace. It was reported that Washington came to Celey Plantation to ask her father if he could court her. Her father refused, saying, "If that is your mission here, sir, you may as well order your horse. My daughter has been accustomed to her coach and six." What Colonel Cary was saying was that position, wealth and power were the prerequisites for Sally's hand—none of which George Washington had at that time.

Another notable event in the plantation's history occurred during and after the Civil War. The owner of the plantation at this time was John Cary Wilson, who had acquired it through inheritance. The house had a vast collection of books obtained during Colonel Cary's trips back and forth to England. Returning from these trips, he would bring back volumes of books to use for teaching his children. In the 1700s, it was well known throughout the Virginia Company that Colonel Cary's library was the largest outside the Collage of William and Mary.

Wilson, who was the principal of the Hampton Military Academy when the war broke out, was commissioned into the army as a major and put in charge of the troops in and around Hampton. During the war, while meeting with General Benjamin Butler concerning his policy of keeping runway slaves at Fort Monroe, Major Cary turned to General Butler and made a personal request, asking to move his library at Celey Plantation to a safer location. General Butler agreed to save the library, saying, "Books neither fed nor clothed an army." The day after making the request, General Butler signed the paperwork to have the library moved to Smithfield for safekeeping. Unfortunately, Hampton was evacuated before the library could be moved. But Butler was a man of this word. In a letter to Major Cary after the Battle of Bethel, General Butler wrote that even though the library had been looted, he was able to collect what he could find and brought the books for safekeeping to Fort Monroe. When the story about General Butler's act of kindness got out, he was asked many times for interviews and for the return of the volumes, but these overtures were declined. After the war, Major Cary received word that a few of his books were found at the Soldier's Home (now the VA Hospital). When Major Cary arrived from his home in Richmond, he could locate just a few books, and the ones he found were defaced. He gathered up all he could find and left.

When the Civil War ended in 1865, some of "Butler's contrabands" settled in this area. They burned the Celey Plantation house to the ground, used the bricks to build fireplace chimneys for their houses and began farming the

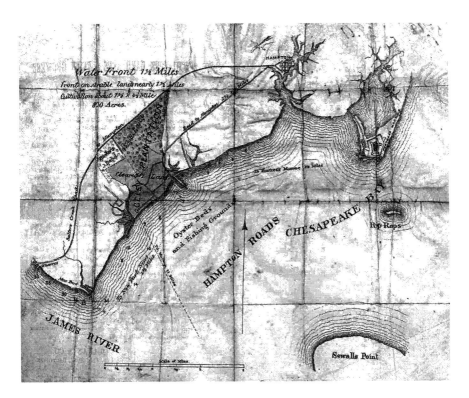

A rare vintage map showing Celey Plantation. *Courtesy of Paul Emigholz.*

Celey House, circa late 1800s. *Courtesy of Greg Siegel.*

land. When William Vaughan, whose wife held interest in the property, came to their land, he found that the squatters had taken up arms to defend their homes. Vaughan called in the sheriff of Elizabeth City County to evict them. However, once he and his small party of men arrived and saw how many squatters there were and how many were armed with guns, he requested that the army commander at Fort Monroe send troops to run the squatters off.

In 1880s, the Celey heirs sold the property to the Newport News, Hampton and Old Point Development Company. The company bought 1,237 acres from Salters Creek to Claremont Avenue and north to the Chesapeake and Ohio railway tracks. It sold twenty-five-foot- by one-hundred-foot lots for the growing industrial workforce. Many families who bought lots in this area bought more than one so that they could establish small farms. They grew crops, raised animals to feed their families and had stables for horses and mules to use as transportation. Later, in the 1930s and '40s, with another housing shortage in the area due to the influx of workers for the increasing number of industrial and government jobs available, the lots that had been used for farming were sold to accommodate more housing. Today, as you walk or drive from Pear Avenue to Orchard Avenue, you can see farmhouses that were part of the original lot sales mixed with houses that were built later.

By 1916, the most populated area of Wythe was concentrated in the area near Salters Creek and the Buxton Hospital, mainly due to the trolley line that began running in 1905 along the Boulevard and the opening of the hospital in 1906. This area was named the Salters Creek Settlement, the Hospital Settlement or the West End Boulevard Settlement, depending on who was addressing the subject. With over 1,100 residents who, for the most part, were employed in Newport News, this group identified more closely with that city than with Elizabeth City County.

In June 1916, a group was formed to petition the courts to incorporate the area as a town under the name of Hampton Roads to separate itself from Elizabeth City County. The name Hampton Roads was denied, but its second choice, Kecoughtan, was accepted by a court order.

The new town of Kecoughtan encompassed roughly the area from Hampton Roads Harbor down to the midpoint of Pear Avenue to the end of Pine Avenue and then followed Salters Creek back to the harbor. The town of Kecoughtan existed for ten years and was given its own section in the Hill's Directory (the local phone book) equal to that of Hampton and Phoebus. The town's government included a mayor, four councilmen, a town sergeant and the Salters Creek Fire Department. The children of

The modern Buxton Hospital. *Courtesy of Greg Siegel.*

the town went to Salters Creek School on Poplar Avenue. In 1922, the Woodrow Wilson School, educating 130 students, replaced it. Both schools were part of the Wythe School System. The students then went to high school at Hampton High. In 1923, a petition with seventy-nine signatures was presented to the court requesting that the entire town of Kecoughtan be annexed to the city of Newport News. In an unusual reversal of roles, it wasn't Newport News asking to acquire the town but rather the citizens of Kecoughtan asking to be annexed to the larger city. This controversial matter was considered by the state court system for two years before a special court of three judges convened in Elizabeth City County. They came to a decision after a trial featuring county supervisors, school officials and residents. On February 23, 1926, the court allowed the town to be annexed to Newport News, causing the Hampton city line to run down the middle of Pear Avenue. The court decreed that Newport News would only acquire the land east to that boundary in Elizabeth City County.

At the time of the Civil War, the middle section of the Wythe neighborhood, today's Indian River Park and the Wythe Crescent/Robinson Park area, was part of George M. Bates's land. Before the Bateses arrived, the entire area was part of Joshua Curle's plantation. Curle's family members were ship captains and merchants/importers. At the time of the Civil War, Bates had purchased a large portion of Joshua Curle's land. Bates, a supporter of the Confederate cause, evacuated his family to Richmond early in the war and died there. His lands were left to his family. In 1873, the Circuit Court appointed special commissioners to divide and sell Bates's land. Most of the land lay undisturbed until 1916, when the Midway Realty Corporation was formed by a group of inventors who had purchased Bates's land. They sold the property to local businessman and developer Charles Hopkins and his partners, one of whom was Allan Jones, a distinguished lawyer in Newport News who went on to build one of the first homes in the development.

Hopkins and his investors formed two companies—Hopkins Land Company, to sell the lots, and the second, the Boulevard Development Corporation, to develop the property. Charles Hopkins was raised in Newport News and had developed housing neighborhoods in New Orleans and in Alabama before coming back to the area to build Indian River Park. In 1922, he moved to Washington, D.C., to develop the Blair and Woodside Park neighborhoods. He settled there and lived out his life until he died there in 1944.

With the local connection to this area's rich Native American history, "Indian River Park" was chosen as the name of the subdivision, and its streets would carry references to this Indian history. After having a survey and plat made of a proposed subdivision, the Boulevard Development Company begin to sell lots to those wanting to build "attractive, high class home places" halfway between Hampton and Newport News. The overalls design included dredging and expanding the existing creek so that small boats could go in and out to the Hampton Roads Harbor. A trolley stop was installed at the intersection of Powhatan Parkway and "the Boulevard" (Chesapeake Avenue), where a five-cent fare would take you to Hampton or Newport News. Amenities included the installation of a sewage system, curbs, sidewalks and streetlights, as well as common areas that were planted with trees and gardens. To keep the streets free of obstructions, alleys were designed behind the homes to handle utilities, telephone lines and trash removal.

From May through December 1916, the developers ran an aggressive advertising campaign in the local newspapers. Over eighty-five ads were placed in the *Times Herald* and the *Daily Press* encouraging citizens to purchase lots and build homes in the planned community. Lots sized 50 by 150 feet sold for $450 to $1,250, depending on location, and a 10 percent down payment was all that was required to purchase the property. At the sales office, located near the Powhatan Parkway Bridge, were lists of preapproved homebuilders and house plans. To ensure that the homes were built to the highest standard, each lot deed specified that the cost of the home must be at least $3,000 and that the development company would have to approve the plans. On the porch of the sales office, rocking chairs were provided so that prospective buyers could sit and appreciate what it would mean to have a home in this neighborhood. Between 1916 and 1920, many of the buyers purchased lots on speculation and did not immediately build on them. By 1945, all the lots within Indian River Park had houses built on them.

To maintain the integrity of Indian River Park, a provision in the lot deeds was made for the permanent upkeep of the property with the formation of the Indian River Park Association (IRPA). Each lot was assessed twenty-five or thirty-five cents per month for this purpose, depending where the lot was located. This homeowners' association was in charge of the maintenance of the lighting, sewage system, streets and common areas. By 1921, there were enough homeowners living in Indian River Park that the Boulevard Development Company turned the association over to its residents. Elections were held and bylaws passed, and the new IRPA was established. By 1940, Elizabeth City County took over this responsibility, and the deed requirement for the assessment fee was eliminated. After World War II, residents of Indian River Park revived the association, which became a volunteer group that worked on quality-of-life issues that affected the neighborhood.

The developers of Indian River Park wanted to make a bold statement at the entrance to the subdivision. An entrance lodge was built on either side of the wooden bridge that spanned Indian River Creek at Powhatan Parkway, which connected the Boulevard (now Chesapeake Avenue) to Kecoughtan Road. The lodges, which were designed to look the same, served as trolley stops for the line that connected Hampton and Newport News. One of the lodges was built to shade passengers from the elements while waiting for the trolley, and the other was built with a pass-through.

Another distinct feature of Indian River Park was its streetlights. These light fixtures were made of cast iron and were originally topped with round globes. In 1925, the IRPA decided to make it easier for people visiting the neighborhood by installing street signs on all cross streets. Signs were purchased from the Lysle Sign Company for a cost of seventy dollars and installed directly on the lampposts. The sign company was so impressed with how the street signs looked that it asked for a description from the IRPA and took photographs to be used in its advertising. Unfortunately, the street signs started to rust due to the salt air. The IRPA contacted the sign company for

-: **STOP OFF AT** :-
INDIAN RIVER PARK

OFFICE

Enjoy the sea cooled breezes. Make yourself at home on the veranda of our office. The comfortable rocking chairs are for your convenience. You will then be able to appreciate what it will mean to you to have a home in this ideal spot.

Hopkins Land Company, Inc.

Silsby Bldg.   Phone 628

An early advertisement offering the sale of Indian River Park property. *Courtesy of Greg Siegel.*

help in solving the problem, even asking for new street signs. The Lysle Sign Company stated that since it had not been made aware of the salt conditions in the area, it was not responsible for the replacement of the signs.

In 1948, the lights received an upgrade as the globes were replaced with Colonial-looking light fixtures made by an IRP resident who worked at the Newport News Shipyard, which was more cost effective than purchasing them from a manufacturer. In 1959, in order to have a more consistent look with other neighborhoods in the area, "Williamsburg"-style light fixtures were bought by the city to replace the Colonial-style fixtures.

On the other side of the western branch of Indian River Creek, surrounding today's Robinson Park, was land owned partly by local businessman Captain John Robinson, who had come to Wythe's shores in 1886. Frank Hooper and George Howe, the owners of the Warwick Iron Works in Newport News, also speculated in land development and other investments in the area. In 1916, the rest of the available land in this area was sold to Hooper and Howe. Their land was directly adjacent to the Robinson land. Hooper and Howe leased their land to a local farmer, who used the area for growing potatoes. In the 1930s, with the increased

One of the Unique Features of

Indian River Park

Will be the Lighting of Harbor
Drive from Pochin Place
to Pocahontas Place.

Harbor Drive will be illuminated
by electric lights in ground glass
globes, topping ornamental iron
standards. These lights around the
winding drive bordering the inland
harbor will have a very pleasing effect
and make the "night time" appearance
of the park most picturesque.

This is but one of the features
that are making this property "the
talk of the town." Let us show you
others.

The selecting of your building site in the Park is a matter that it
would be well for you to take up without delay, that is if choice of location is a consideration to you.

LARGE LOTS   50x150 With All Improvements
$450 to $1250

Boulevard Development Corporation
Owners
HOPKINS LAND CO., Inc.
Sales Agents
Basement Bixby Bldg. .... Phone 828

A 1916 *Daily Press* advertisement highlighting the state-of-the-art
streetlights in Indian River Park. *Courtesy of Greg Siegel.*

demand for housing in the area, Robinson, Hooper and Howe worked
together to plot out lots to develop new homes on their land.

In August 1935, during the layout of this new development, Robinson,
Hopper and Howe offered a three-and-a-half-acre plot of land to the
Elizabeth City County supervisors for a park to be named the John C.
Robinson Park, and the county willingly accepted. While the park area was
being leveled and cleared, a grave site was found in the area where today

sits the memorial monument to Officer Kenny Wallace. This grave site, reportedly lined with bricks, most likely held the remains of the Bates family. Captain Robinson took the remains to Greenlawn Cemetery and had them interred there, paying for the grave site out of his own pocket.

For years, stories of the park being home to an Indian grave site or connected to the Indians because of its arrowhead shape have circulated, but they are just tales, as no definitive information backing up the stories has ever been substantiated. Robinson Park has changed little from what it looked when it was first opened. The smaller trees that were left for shade have grown into huge shade trees, although some have fallen during storms or have been taken down due to rot. The City of Hampton has worked to plant new ones to keep the park looking as the original developers envisioned it. The original park pavilion was removed by the City of Hampton, owing to its deteriorated condition. The original playground equipment was removed in the 1950s, but new state-of-the-art equipment was placed back in the park in 2010.

After the Civil War, in the area from LaSalle Avenue to East Avenue, homes were built on farmland once owned by Daniel Cumming. More homes were constructed once the trolley line was opened along the Boulevard and LaSalle Avenue, connecting with the line on Electric Avenue, now Victoria Boulevard.

In 1916, homes started to be built from the harbor inward along open spaces around the Hampton Roads Golf Course. Dirt roads were made, and homes were built along these lanes. Once the golf course was closed in 1922, the Armstrong Land Company plotted roads between East Avenue and Hampton Roads Avenue. Armstrong divided the land into lots to sell to builders and individuals alike. Most of the homes in this area were built in the 1930s and early 1940s. When you travel these streets, you can easily pick out homes that were built by the same builders as opposed to the more unique homes.

Named by the *Daily Press* as one of the top ten spots to enjoy a walk in the Hampton Roads area, Olde Wythe is today a vibrant, historic neighborhood with over 1,400 distinctly different home styles that make it stand out from other neighborhoods in the area. With its character and charm, the Olde Wythe welcome mat is always out to greet visitors and new homeowners.

Chapter 2

HAMPTON'S COLONIAL HERO, GEORGE WYTHE

The most historically significant native of Hampton was George Wythe. An influential advocate of American independence and a signer of the Declaration of Independence, a delegate to the Constitutional Convention, an important politician and lawyer, a deeply learned and widely reputed teacher and judge, and a role model for an austere and civically responsible lifestyle, Wythe's greatest attribute was his opposition to the enslavement of human beings. While many Virginians claimed to oppose slavery but actually lived idly and prosperously from the toil of enslaved African Americans, George Wythe freed his slaves during his lifetime. He was condemned and even socially shunned for his principled position, but he never wavered.

Wythe was born in 1726 on Chesterville, a prosperous plantation in what was then Elizabeth City County, at the head of navigability of the northwest branch of the Back River. Now a part of the NASA Langley Research Center, the ruins of his birthplace can be visited only with special permission from NASA Langley. Born to Thomas Wythe III and Margaret Walker Wythe, members of the gentry, he had an older brother, Thomas IV, and a sister, Anne. His faithful servant, Lydia Brodnax, was born at Chesterville around 1742. Although Wythe set her free in 1787, she cooked and kept house for her good friend until he died.

The first Thomas Wythe had settled in Virginia in 1680 and quickly became politically and socially prominent, serving both as a justice of the peace on the Elizabeth City County Court and in the House of Burgesses. He purchased the first 204 acres of Chesterville (containing a manor house)

Left: Bust of George Wythe. *Courtesy of Hampton History Museum.*

Below: Chesterville. *Courtesy of NASA Langley.*

from Edmund Sweeney in 1691. Thomas II also sat as a county justice and became one of Hampton's first trustees, or founders, but he died suddenly at age twenty-four in 1694, only one month after his father. Thomas III served in the House of Burgesses, was briefly county sheriff, and then took the family seat on the county court. He also owned a half interest in a commercial wharf in the port town and tobacco entrepôt that Hampton was rapidly becoming. He did not survive his thirties, however, dying when his younger son, George, was three and leaving Chesterville to Thomas IV.

Receiving slaves and a fine family name from his father, young George would find his future shaped much more by the strong influence of his mother. Margaret Wythe's grandfather had been the redoubtable and charismatic George Keith, who held an MA from Marischal College in his native Aberdeen, Scotland, where he studied mathematics and oriental languages and became a vigorous opponent of slavery. Keith then spent thirty years spreading the Quaker faith to America. He was later disowned by the Quakers, became an Anglican, and returned to America in 1702 to proclaim his new faith, preaching in Williamsburg the following year.

As a Quaker, Keith had educated his daughters, a very unusual occurrence for English-speaking women at the time. One of them, Anne, married George Walker, a pilot, customs agent, gunner, and storekeeper at the fort at Old Point Comfort, which guarded the entrance to Hampton Roads and the James River, and lived with him at Strawberry Banks. In 1708, Anne won a legal battle against the Quaker Walker, allowing her to rear their children as Anglicans. She passed on to the children much of the learning she had acquired, so daughter Margaret Walker Wythe was able to instruct her son George in the rudiments of mathematics, logic, grammar, Latin, and Greek. After her death, he completed his education at the Grammar School of the College of William and Mary.

Margaret gave her son a lifelong devotion to learning. Wythe's judicial opinions are peppered with untranslated Latin and Greek phrases, and he began to acquire Hebrew in his seventies. His large book collection, which he had given to his friend Thomas Jefferson, helped form the basis of the first Library of Congress, which was burned by the British in 1814. As a man of the Enlightenment, Wythe was knowledgeable in mathematics, natural sciences, political economy, history, and modern languages, as well as imbued with the science and traditions of the law. George also inherited the resolute feistiness and adherence to principle characteristic of his grandmother Walker and his great-grandfather Keith. He would replicate the latter's steadfast opposition to slavery.

Soon Wythe went off to Charles City County to study law under his uncle Stephen Dewey. A busy practitioner, Dewey neglected his charge, confining Wythe to drudgeries and allowing legal instruction to fall by the wayside. After two tedious years, Wythe returned to Chesterville to finish his preparation. At twenty, he took the bar examination in Williamsburg, which was given orally by other lawyers. One of his four inquisitors was Dewey; another was Peyton Randolph, who eventually became the first president of the uniting colonies' First Continental Congress. Wythe passed easily and was licensed to practice law by the Elizabeth City County Court on June 18, 1746, probably around his twentieth birthday.

He began practicing in Spotsylvania County, where he worked in the Fredericksburg office of Zachary Lewis, the King's Attorney. Wythe was soon admitted to the bar in at least three adjoining counties and began a lucrative practice. Learned and thoroughly prepared rather than skilled in cross examination, today he would be better suited to appellate courts rather than trials by jury. The day after Christmas 1747, Wythe wedded Anne Lewis, Zachary's daughter. The bride died suddenly on August 8 of the following year, probably because of a complicated pregnancy. Disconsolate, Wythe drowned himself in drink.

Soon pulling himself together, he moved to Williamsburg, the colony's capital, which was full of good lawyers, academic discussions, and interesting politics. Wythe became clerk of two powerful standing committees of the House of Burgesses and was admitted to the bars of York and Warwick Counties (and probably other nearby counties such as James City). He was soon hired by members of the powerful and influential Blair, Custis, and Fitzhugh families, and eventually his clients included George Washington, Richard Henry Lee, and one of Virginia's wealthiest planters, Robert Carter III. George Wythe would not accept the case of a client who lied to him, returning the full fees of those he discovered had been false, and he would not accept a case he thought no one could win. He earned a spotless reputation for honesty, good ethics and integrity.

Inevitably, Wythe entered politics and was elected as one of six aldermen for Williamsburg in 1750. From their number, the aldermen selected a mayor, and Wythe served in that capacity from 1768 until 1771. To Governor Dinwiddie's disgust, because of his reputation for personal integrity, Wythe was chosen by the Burgesses as auditor of the more than £60,000 they appropriated in 1753 and 1754 to fight the French and Indian War.

The King's Attorney, Peyton Randolph, was required by the House of Burgesses to travel to London to protest the governor's demand to be paid one pistole (about $240 today) for every land grant he signed. There was a large backlog of unsigned grants, and title was not perfect without the signature, so the governor expected to profit handsomely. The Burgesses demanded that they be asked to vote on any revenue the government wanted to exact from the people. Colonials were not represented in Parliament. The cry of "no taxation without representation" would be raised frequently thereafter.

Insulted, Dinwiddie claimed that Randolph had forfeited his position and appointed Wythe as the King's Attorney, despite the many reputable attorneys older than he, since Wythe's legal opinion was that the governor had the power he claimed, and for him (unlike most others) the law did not yield to political upset. Placed in a delicate position, Wythe assured his angry friends that he would resign when Randolph returned.

The year 1755 would prove a memorable one for George Wythe. His brother Thomas died without children, so he inherited Chesterville and assumed the "Wythe seat" on Elizabeth City County's governing court. Randolph returned from England, bringing back a vague agreement that the governor's power to tax would be limited, so Wythe dutifully resigned. And Wythe fell in love with and married Elizabeth Taliaferro, a woman probably half his age. The wealthy Taliaferros lived at Powhatan, a plantation not five miles from Williamsburg, and Elizabeth's father, Richard, the colony's best architect, designed and built the couple a fine brick house located between the Governor's Palace and Bruton Parish Church. The couple lived happily there—still known today as the "Wythe House"—until Elizabeth's unfortunate death in 1787. In the 1770s, perhaps with the help of his architect friends, Thomas Jefferson, or his father-in-law, Wythe built himself and Elizabeth a new house at Chesterville; however, he never seems to have made it their home. The ruins of this house are also visible today at NASA Langley.

In 1758, Francis Fauquier became governor of Virginia and thus the Wythes' neighbor. Also that year, William Small arrived as William and Mary's new professor of natural philosophy (today known as "science"). Fauquier was a learned man, a fellow of London's Royal Society, and a published political economist. The three became fast friends, dining together and debating the great political and scientific questions of the day. When seventeen-year-old Thomas Jefferson matriculated at William and Mary in 1760, he was welcomed into this invigorating intellectual company. The good times ended when, in 1764, Small returned to Scotland and Jefferson completed his study of law with Wythe.

Wythe exhibited continuing interest in scientific endeavors, performing experiments in his home. As he had with Jefferson, Wythe often took promising young men into his home to educate them; poverty-stricken William Munford in the 1780s was given instruction without charge, and Wythe acquired scientific equipment to teach him physics. Munford would move with Wythe to Richmond when the latter left Williamsburg in 1791; he would later become clerk of the House of Delegates, reporter for Virginia's Court of Appeals and a distinguished author.

Among the many improved by Wythe's educational efforts were Bermuda-born St. George Tucker, a legal treatise writer who succeeded Wythe as professor of law at William and Mary, was appointed to Virginia's Court of Appeals, and later became federal district judge for Eastern Virginia; John Marshall, Jefferson's rival and for more than thirty years Chief Justice of the U.S. Supreme Court; Spencer Roane, a Virginia delegate and senator who later sat on the benches of Virginia's General Court and Court of Appeals; John Breckinridge, member of the House of Representatives, the U.S. Senate from Kentucky, and U.S. Attorney General under Jefferson; Littleton Waller Tazewell, member of the House of Delegates and the federal House of Representatives, a U.S. senator, and governor of Virginia; and Henry Clay, U.S. senator from Kentucky, Speaker of the House of Representatives, U.S. Secretary of State, and losing candidate for the presidency in 1824, 1832, and 1844.

At first, Wythe taught students individually. But in 1779, Jefferson, now Virginia's governor, had the legislature create for him a Chair of Law and Police at William and Mary. Wythe thereby became the second lecturer in common law at a university in any English-speaking country, following the eminent William Blackstone at Oxford. Wythe had a broader conception of legal education than is usual today; embodied in the word "police" in his title (meaning "political science"), he saw his duty as the education of judges and legislators, not merely legal practitioners. He taught history, economics, and politics as well as legal rules and processes and was probably the first person to teach constitutional law. Wythe used the moot court, during which his students attempted to argue both sides of cases he made up. He also created a unique institution: every Saturday, his students engaged in a moot legislature, debating the merits of bills before the General Assembly. Both activities had citizens of the town as spectators, as they occurred in the now-disused capitol building's courtroom.

Wythe excelled at teaching governance to legal fledglings since he served in almost every office and participated in momentous decisions during the long fight for independence and the creation of governments for the new republic. He was elected Burgess for the College of William and

St. George
Tucker. *Courtesy of
Hampton History Museum.*

Mary in 1758 and was assigned to membership in three important House committees. In 1761, he finally won election to represent Elizabeth City County, which had denied him a victory in 1756. He was named to the committee that instructed Virginia's permanent representative in London, Edward Montague, as relations with England deteriorated.

Wythe opposed the state's Two Penny Act, which cut by two-thirds the compensation paid to the established Anglican clergy. The act eventually passed; however, the reverend ministers roundly protested, and King George II disallowed it in 1759, whereupon several sued for their back pay. In 1763, as a member of the Elizabeth City County Court, he overruled a jury verdict in favor of the Reverend Thomas Warrington. Despite Wythe's opposition to the pay cut, the Two Penny Act was now Virginia's law, and Wythe enforced whatever that law was. He felt that the king and the British government had no right to interfere with Virginia's internal laws, so that King George's veto was not the law.

The British did not abandon their policy of charging the rising costs of empire against the colonials who formed the most prosperous part of that empire. A Stamp Act was drafted in 1764 that would place a tax on every piece of paper in the colonies, as Montague wearily informed the Virginia House of Burgesses. The House produced letters of opposition, and Wythe, charged with writing to the House of Commons, said angrily that "it is essential to British liberty that laws imposing taxes on the people ought not to be made without the consent of representatives chosen" by those who would know local circumstances and are to the pay the tax.

Commons refused to receive Wythe's letter, and approved the Stamp Act in March 1765. Near the end of the Burgesses' next session on May 30, when two-thirds of the members had left town, Patrick Henry obtained passage of five fiery resolutions against the act, despite the opposition of Wythe and several others who thought them too incendiary. Henry, however, spoke for many colonials, and Committees of Correspondence grew up in every colony to coordinate opposition to stamped paper. Most stamp tax officials were intimidated into resigning. Britain repealed the act in March 1766 but fulminated that it could tax the colonials "in all cases whatsoever."

Governor Fauquier died in 1768. He had been well liked by Virginians, but his two successors, Lords Botetourt and Dunmore, were less tractable as conditions became more strained. Wythe clashed openly with Dunmore, most notably when the governor was sitting as judge in the General Court. Wythe and Robert Carter Nicholas were attorneys on one side, the other represented by Edmund Pendleton. A postponement was requested since Pendleton's associate was missing, but Dunmore denied it, arrogantly chuckling, "Go on, Mr. Pendleton. You'll be a match for both of them." Wythe riposted angrily, "With your Lordship's assistance!" The governor reddened and glared at the obstreperous colonial.

Wythe eventually concluded that he could no longer support the king except as a figurehead leader of a group of independent states. Parliament, for Wythe and his fellow radicals, could not legislate for any of those states except Great Britain, nor could it interfere with a colony's internal affairs or trade. Opposition based on these emerging principles grew vigorously. Wythe had left the House in 1768 when he was appointed clerk, so he did not engage in the stirring debates or vote on the continued assertions of Virginia's rights—but he did what he could to aid the cause. In 1769, the Burgesses were composing an appeal to the king against the ministry's policies when Governor Botetourt demanded that the House's clerk provide him with its minutes. Wythe delayed in replying to the governor until the Burgesses finished their work, preventing the House's dissolution before the protest was completed. Botetourt did eventually dissolve it, but its members continued to meet extra-legally at the Raleigh Tavern, agreeing to a general colonial boycott of certain British goods.

In 1774, Wythe was elected to Virginia's Committee of Safety, a shadow Patriot agency that Dunmore could not dissolve. Another revolutionary body was the Virginia Convention, elected by the people as their sovereign representative, which met in Williamsburg beginning in August 1774 to establish Virginia policy. The first Convention selected delegates to the First Continental Congress, which finally joined together all thirteen American colonies. When the Congress met in Philadelphia later that year, among those attending were George Washington, Peyton Randolph, Patrick Henry, Edmund Pendleton, Richard Henry Lee, and George Wythe.

Tensions heightened after British regulars, given secret orders to capture local colonial military supplies, fired on Massachusetts Minutemen at Lexington on April 19, 1775. In Virginia, Lord Dunmore followed the same orders, seizing the colony's supply of gunpowder in Williamsburg and scurrying aboard a British warship in Hampton Roads. Outraged, Wythe took a musket, donned a buckskin hunting shirt—the "uniform" of the Patriots—and joined the militia parade of protest. The British attacked Norfolk and Hampton in October 1775 but were driven off ignominiously by Virginia's own Minutemen. Early in 1776, Dunmore finally fled, taking with him many Loyalists and their families.

Meanwhile, George and Elizabeth Wythe set off for the Second Continental Congress, which met in September 1775. George, who would remain in Philadelphia through momentous times until June 1776, supported free trade for the colonials and demanded, "We must declare ourselves a free People...The Safety of America depends essentially on a Union of the People in it." He was leading the charge for full independence by February 1776, joined by other radicals such as John and Sam Adams and Ben Franklin. Virginia concurred with a formal call for independence in May, and Congress agreed by vote on July 2, with Thomas Jefferson's resounding Declaration being approved two days later. By then, Wythe and Richard Henry Lee had returned home to help adopt a republican form of government in the Old Dominion. The Virginia delegation honored Wythe's steadfast leadership toward independence by leaving a space at the top of their signatures on the Declaration for his, when he returned to Congress in late summer.

Carried in Wythe's pocket, Jefferson's draft ideas for Virginia's new government were only partially adopted, as most of the suggestions were much too progressive; he wanted manumission for slaves, separation from the Anglican Church, free education for all, and a broader franchise. Jefferson and Wythe would spend a decade seeking these reforms plus a revised judiciary, freedom of religion, public access to records, and a much more liberal criminal code. They achieved some of what they desired when, in 1776, the Commonwealth appointed them to a committee to revise Virginia's laws to accord with the letter and spirit of the new constitution, and when, the next year, Wythe became the powerful Speaker of the House of Delegates. More would eventually be enacted, but this was his last stint in Virginia's legislature, as he soon ascended the bench. Before Washington defeated the British at Yorktown in 1781, he stayed with George and Elizabeth Wythe in Williamsburg; Chesterville, with its rabid Tory groundskeeper, was dangerously close to the action.

In January 1778, Wythe took his seat as one of the three judges on Virginia's new Court of Chancery, along with Pendleton and Nicholas. Chancery gave litigants relief when the common-law courts could give none. Sitting alone after 1789 because of another reform of the judiciary, Wythe would remain Chancellor until his death. There he sat, incorruptible, in the words of a worshipful student, "a judge uncontaminated by prejudice or partiality, or meaner selfishness, he held the even scales of justice well balanced in his hands."

A final political activity, however, had to be undertaken by Wythe when it seemed to many that the Articles of Confederation had not created a sufficiently strong and decisive national government. Elected to the Constitutional Convention, he was chosen its parliamentarian and established the rules of procedure by which his colleagues would debate and determine a new fundamental governance document. The illness of Elizabeth Wythe called him home after a month in Philadelphia; she perished in August, and the heartbroken Wythe did not return. As a Federalist, Wythe strongly supported the new governmental blueprint when it came before Virginia's Ratification Convention in June 1788, serving as chair of the Committee of the Whole, where all the important debates occurred. There were trenchant arguments that the new edifice was too centralized, and opponents included Patrick Henry, George Mason, and James Monroe. Wythe's sole speech, one of the last made, moved for adoption, noting the necessity of the reforms it portended and that amendments should be proposed only after adoption. Despite brilliant rebuttal by Henry, the motion passed 89–79, and

Virginia had ratified the new governance document. Wythe then proposed forty amendments, which were also approved.

Signature of George Wythe on the Declaration of Independence. *Courtesy of Hampton History Museum.*

As a judge, Wythe gave opinions in many important cases. In November 1782, he sat with seven other members of the Court of Appeals in *Caton v. Commonwealth.* John Caton and two other Loyalists had been convicted of treason and sentenced to death. The House of Delegates issued pardons, but the Senate failed to concur. Virginia's constitution gave the right of pardon to the House alone, but a directly conflicting state statute allowed pardons with the consent of both houses. Attorney General Edmund Randolph argued that the statute controlled—without Senate approval, the pardons were invalid. Further, he said, given the doctrine of separation of powers, the court had no power to declare the statute void. Six members of the court accepted Randolph's first argument but ignored the crucial constitutional question. Dissenter James Mercer, who found the pardons good, flatly declared that the statute was unconstitutional. Wythe thought the pardons valid but, in eloquent dicta, spoke of the judicial duty "to protect the community against the usurpations" of a legislative body ignoring constitutional boundaries. "In administering the public justice of the country," he would "point to the constitution [and] say to them [the legislature], here is the limit of your authority; and hither, shall you go, but no further." An attentive young John Marshall was in the large audience.

In 1793, Wythe courageously gave his quite unpopular opinion on the British debts. Millions of dollars were owed by large numbers of Virginians to British merchants when Virginia's courts ceased operations in 1774 because of the impending break with England. The courts remained closed to suits to recover these debts through eight desperate years of Revolution. Under legislation drafted by Jefferson, the state confiscated all the "British debts," as they came to be called. Virginians could "pay off" such debts by tendering the greatly depreciated paper money the state emitted during the conflict to a loan office established by the state, allowing the elimination of large amounts of debt with very little of actual value and, since the state had sovereign immunity, effectively preventing any collection of the debts. Wythe availed himself of the scheme, yet he did not later recuse himself from hearing a case challenging the legality of these measures. Article IV of the Treaty of Paris, ending the Revolution, provided that British creditors would meet with no legal impediments to the collection of prewar debts, and the shady Virginia loan office scheme was perhaps the best example of such a legal impediment.

Many Virginians believed that victory had cancelled their debts to the hated British. Further, the devastation wrought by British armies had ruined much of the farms, cattle, crops, and other resources by which repayment could be financed. Additionally, a decade-long depression commencing around 1781 had made it almost impossible to make payments in silver, as the treaty required. These points were well argued by counsel when Wythe heard *Page v. Pendleton.*

Wythe angrily wrote that "rhetoric [was] copiously poured forth…in order to prove that an American citizen might honestly as well as profitably with[h]old money which he owed to a British subject." Victory in the war had not cancelled any debts, he ruled, for a contract was a contract; mere circumstances, such as the British destruction of agricultural resources, made no difference. Further, the new U.S. Constitution made all treaties the supreme law of the land, so that Article IV abrogated any Virginia law to the contrary (such as the loan office scheme). Civilization meant "to deal faithfully." His apoplectic friends and neighbors might owe more than they could pay, but for Wythe, deliberate failure to meet proven obligations was "barbarism." In his anger, he completely omitted responding to the political and contextual arguments made by the debtors. Wythe was hurriedly reversed by the Court of Appeals, which was listening to the rising debtor clamor; however, in a separate case in 1796, the U.S. Supreme Court agreed with him.

Wythe and his eminent contemporary Edmund Pendleton were longtime rivals. When Virginia reorganized its court system in 1789, elevating Wythe's two colleagues on the chancery court to a new Court of Appeals staffed with its own five judges, it made Pendleton the state's Chief Justice and left Wythe alone as Chancellor. More than 150 cases decided by Wythe were appealed, and perhaps the majority were modified or reversed, mostly through Pendleton's efforts. Wythe got so exasperated that he began openly criticizing Pendleton in his opinions, and in 1795 he published a volume containing his decisions, some of which bitterly attacked his tormentor.

Another controversial issue tackled by Wythe was the fate of the glebe lands, set aside by the former colony in each Anglican parish to support a minister. The state disestablished the church in 1786 but still owned the glebes. After years of wrangling, a statute of 1802 empowered local officials to sell these lands. The Episcopal Church objected, appealing to the Chancellor to enjoin any sales. In *Turpin v. Lockett*, Wythe again acted contrary to the desires of his neighbors, holding the statute constitutional. Another appeal followed, but Chief Justice Pendleton died the night before he could deliver an opinion reversing Wythe. With only four of the five judges participating, Pendleton's replacement, St. George Tucker, joined Spencer Roane in voting to uphold Wythe's ruling, thereby creating a 2–2 tie that affirmed the judgment below and allowed the glebes to be sold.

Having moved to Richmond, the aging Wythe could be seen on Shockoe Hill "not infrequently of a bright frosty morning, in loose array, taking an air bath on the porch of his humble residence." After Elizabeth's death, he adopted plain Quaker-like clothing, ate a spartan vegetarian diet, and acted on his hatred of human enslavement. He deeded back to Elizabeth's relatives thirteen slaves that she had brought to their marriage and began manumitting his own. Lydia Brodnax was first, in October 1787, and five others followed. Wythe also purchased an intelligent mulatto boy, Michael Brown, and manumitted him in the 1790s. Wythe's persistent antislavery actions and many of his judicial opinions were contrary to the interests of Virginia's elites, and some smirked that Wythe had fallen into "disarrangement of his apparel," that he was "senile," that he had been quietly requested to resign by the governor, and even that Brown was his and Lydia's miscegenous son.

Most whites in Virginia's culture could not imagine terminating slavery. The institution gave too much economic and social benefit to wealthy or even middling whites—no backbreaking labor in the fields, no building those magnificent houses. They obtained sustenance and much leisure and luxury from the sweat and toil of slaves. Even poor whites on small farms who owned nobody felt worthwhile because they were not slaves. Wythe did not set anyone free in the many cases coming before him that involved slaves as items of property. But in two suits, the issue of freedom was raised directly by litigants, and Wythe's courage was again exemplified in the two opinions he gave, which were intended to destroy slavery.

Relatives of Quakers John Pleasants and his son Jonathan challenged the provisions in their wills requiring them to free all slaves they inherited when each slave attained the age of thirty. Though manumission was illegal when the wills were written, six years after the younger Pleasants died Virginia enacted a statute in 1782 allowing owners to free their bondsmen. In *Pleasants v. Pleasants* (1799), Wythe cut through many legal knots to order that more than four hundred "men, women and children detained in slavery" be granted "restitution" of their freedom. Wythe found that each of the Pleasants had impressed his property with a trust requiring emancipation whenever the legislature granted that privilege. Moreover, though the wills did not say so, Wythe declared that children born to mothers freed after 1782 were free from birth. In an even more revolutionary holding, Wythe ordered years of "back wages" for the Pleasants' slaves who should have been set free in 1782.

In a second case that was probably heard late in 1805, Jackie Wright petitioned Wythe for freedom. She and her children, long enslaved, claimed that they were Indians, not African Americans. Slaves had but one statutory right in Virginia, to prove they were free, but they had to overcome a legal presumption that they were properly enslaved. Wright argued that her maternal line of descent was entirely through Indians and that no "Negro blood" had seeped into her veins since the time of her free Native American great-grandmother. In *Wrights v. Hudgins*, Wythe ruled that the Wrights were free. First, they were all in court, and Wythe observed no markers of Negro descent. Second, the initial article of Virginia's Bill of Rights declared that "all men are by nature equally free." This meant, to the great Chancellor, that each human possessed freedom as an inherent right. When the Bill of Rights was legislatively debated, hedges had been supposedly inserted to prevent blacks from making this very claim of right, but Wythe ignored the hedges, resting his judgment upon the ringing words. He thereby forced white Virginians to confront the humanity of their slaves and the inhumanity of their treatment in the context of their Revolutionary demand for their own freedom. Wythe's two rulings could shake slavery to its foundations. It was his greatest moment—directly challenging the heart of Virginia's brutality.

On appeal, Wythe's decrees of freedom for the two sets of enslaved persons were affirmed, but the horrified Court of Appeals reversed him on his slavery-threatening legal rulings. Particularly overturned were his decision on "back pay," the holding that babies born to freed Pleasants slaves were immediately free, and his bold interpretation of the Bill of Rights. The institution of slavery was not to be challenged. Economics was much more important than ideology.

Both of Wythe's opinions were met with public outrage, and they might have contributed to his murder. For on May 25, 1806, Wythe and two freed slaves in his household, Brodnax and young Brown, came down with arsenic poisoning. Brown died immediately, Wythe lingered for two pain-filled weeks, and Brodnax eventually recovered. The fourth household member, Wythe's great-nephew George Wythe Sweeney, the principal taker under his will, was accused of murder. Arsenic was found in his room. The young rake had stolen from his guardian, had forged checks in his name, and probably resented the legacies Wythe left to Brown and Brodnax. (The old man was able to disinherit Sweeney before he died.) Wythe was autopsied, after his deathbed request, but two white doctors, both slaveholders, failed to run arsenic tests. The jury acquitted Sweeney because of the doctors' omission, plus the inadmissibility of Brodnax's eyewitness testimony (she saw Sweeney put powder into the stewpot)—blacks could not testify against whites. Even a reprobate white man was apparently not going to hang in slaveholding Virginia either for the murder of a black youth or for the murder of the most vocal opponent of slavery in his time.

Chapter 3

AMATEUR HISTORY HUNTING
YIELDS ARTIFACTS

Throughout the years, stories of Indians and early seventeenth- and eighteenth-century Virginians living in the area now known as Wythe have led residents to search for evidence to back up such stories.

After the Civil War, this area changed from one with very little habitation and development to one where many northerners, looking for investments and a chance to start anew, bought land for what was owed in back taxes. With this new beginning, people began to build homes along the harbor. Soon after, many of the new residents began to record finding Indian relics and early seventeenth-century artifacts.

One of the families who settled here after the Civil War was the Robinson family, who came from Massachusetts in 1874. One of their sons, John Cutler or J.C., who was fourteen at the time, eventually became a successful oysterman known as Captain Robinson, an entrepreneur, a community leader and a landowner in Wythe. While a teenager and into his adulthood, J.C. loved to uncover the past. He would become known as an amateur archaeologist in the area with his collections of Indian artifacts and with the research he would undertake in studying the Indians and how they lived. In all, J.C. found hundreds of Indian artifacts and displayed them in his home office.

In a 1935 interview in which he discussed his findings, Captain Robinson stated that he concluded that Indians traveled to the shores of Olde Wythe to set up camp for fishing and hunting. He based this conclusion on the

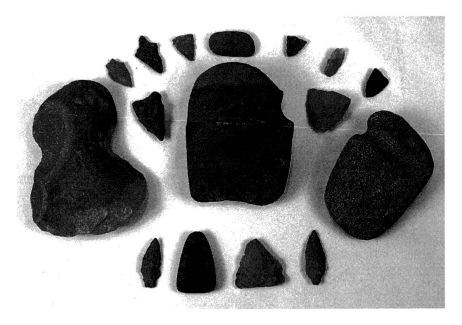

A portion of Captain John Cutler Robinson's collection of Indian artifacts. *Courtesy of Hampton History Museum.*

fact that the arrowheads and spearheads found were made from stone not found in this region and therefore must have been brought from afar. Captain Robinson went on to say that it was reported to him that this area had been known for its population of deer and other animals for hunting. He speculated that the Indians would take their food back to their villages, located farther up the James River. Captain Robinson was not the only member of his family to find Indian artifacts. Many of his relatives who lived in the area also found numerous artifacts while cultivating their gardens. After Captain Robinson's death, his collection of artifacts was gifted to the Hampton History Museum.

Others have reported finding arrowheads and other items associated with the Indians on Captain Robinson's land. Fred Ferrari, who lived on Electric Avenue (now Victoria Boulevard) in the 1920s, shared the following story. As a young boy, Fred would walk from his home to the harbor to swim, fish and just have fun. To get to the harbor, he would walk though what is now Robinson Park. At the time, part of this land was leased to a potato farmer. While cutting through the plowed field, Fred would look down and see arrowheads lying on top of the soil. He would pick up some to keep for himself and leave behind others, as he had no interest in collecting them.

Even today, you can still uncover artifacts from the past. Mr. and Mrs. Gene Carter of Claremont Avenue have, while gardening, collected many artifacts over the years, including arrowheads, pieces of dishes that looked old and even a spoon. After showing the artifacts to an archaeologist, it was determined that the small pieces of dishes were from the mid-nineteenth century. One piece could have been from a saucer or a plate and the other from teacup or bowl. The spoon they found turned out to be a promotional gift given out by a Standard Oil Company gas station in 1960.

One Sunday afternoon in 1940, the discovery of artifacts in Wythe took a turn that brought notoriety to the area from the Mariners' Museum in Newport News to the Smithsonian Institution in Washington, D.C. The story begins with two brothers, Alvin and Joe Brittingham, who lived across from each other in the 130 block of LaSalle Avenue. Alvin ran the family furniture business in downtown Hampton, while Joe worked at the Newport News Shipyard. On most Sunday afternoons after church and lunch, the brothers and some of their children would take walks around the area. While walking along the banks of the harbor near Church Creek on this particular Sunday, which followed a day of heavy rain, the group found a bone sticking out of the bank. Thinking at first that it was a tree root, the men dug around the object and saw that whatever it was, it was getting bigger and longer. Further digging led the men to uncover what appeared to be a human bone. After placing a call to the police, who came and took the bone with them, the Brittinghams and their friends began to speculate on what they had found. Could it be Blackbeard, the famous pirate? Was it the remains of a sailor who fell overboard from a navy ship that came through the harbor? Although they never found out, this bone stirred their curiosity.

With Alvin busy running the furniture store and taking care of his mother, Joe studied books about the techniques and tools used in archaeological searches, including one tool called a sounding rod. The sounding rod was twisted into the ground, and its threads would catch material when pulled up to the surface. Alvin and Joe made their own sounding rod to use in their search. Theirs was made from a steel bar, three-eighths inch in diameter by three and a half feet long, with a twelve-inch wooden T-handle bolted on the top. Toward the bottom, they machined threads into the steel bar like a corkscrew.

Alvin Brittingham studying the area of the 1940 dig, 1946. *Courtesy of Virginia Department of Historic Resources.*

The brothers first concentrated their search behind LaSalle Avenue, along Church Creek. After each heavy rainfall, they would walk the area looking for artifacts that had risen to the surface and pick up anything they thought was interesting. Using their sounding rod, they pulled up such items as oyster shells and pieces of brick and pottery.

In August 1940, Joe and Alvin began exploring the east side of Church Creek and found an area that contained numerous brick shale pieces, which they thought had been brought to the surface after repeated plowings when the area was used as a farm. They surmised this was some sort of a building foundation.

Working in the area where the first brick pieces were found, the brothers used the sounding rod to bring up more and more pieces of brick. This led to their first "dig," in which they uncovered a large fireplace foundation. After more digging, they discovered that the fireplace's opening faced east, with narrow "wings" existing on both sides. Using the location of the fireplace, the brothers dug trenches to see how big the fireplace's building was and whether it had a brick or wooden foundation. They could not determine the size of the building but concluded that it had to be very large, based on the size of the uncovered fireplace foundation. They also discovered the building had timber sills supported on wooden blocks like many early colonial structures they had researched.

With the discovery of the fireplace, the brothers became interested in learning more about the early settlers and Indians in the Kicotan region. They learned how early settlers and Indians disposed of waste material, such as food remains, broken items and other things. The brothers discovered that homeowners would dig garbage pits, called middens, close to their dwellings. The discarded items were mixed with soil in the middens. The first midden they found was four feet deep and nine feet in diameter. In it, they found pieces of imported pottery, a brass candlestick and various types of Indian relics. After this first midden was excavated, they found several others in the area around the fireplace, uncovering pieces of a Dutch oven and a limekiln, among other things. These finds led to an expanded search and the discovery of a larger assortment of artifacts.

Because of work and family obligations, the excavation was completed during the brothers' free time, mainly on weekends. With a limited schedule, digging became more of a hobby that was shared with family and friends. Alvin's home had a huge garage in back, which included an upstairs room that was used for get-togethers with family and friends. Alvin built shelves around the room on which to display the artifacts they found. This room quickly became a small museum to showcase the items. The brothers loved to show off their finds and tell the stories of how they found them to anyone who showed an interest.

With such a large discovery of early colonial items, along with Indian artifacts from the fireplace site, Alvin and Joe contacted the National Park Service archaeological department at Jamestown. Mr. J.C. Harrington, one of the staff members, took an interest in the project, visited the area and looked at the artifacts. Mr. Harrington told the brothers that, in his opinion, the site was contemporary with the first settlers at Jamestown, and the artifacts that they had found were from the early colonial period. He went on to say that the site should be preserved for further study, if possible. Several well-known Hampton citizens were contacted, shown the artifacts and informed of Mr. Harrington's opinion. A meeting was held to discuss the preservation of the area. Unfortunately, not enough public interest in the project could be raised in order to preserve the site from development.

In the summer of 1941, the brothers continued digging at the same time survey work was being completed for Sussex Hampton, a new housing development for defense workers that would be built over a large portion of their search area. Alvin and Joe knew time was short, so they sped up their exploration, hastily removing the relics without recording details before construction started.

One area in which Joe took a particular interest was a nearby mound of dirt. Hoping to find an Indian burial site, Joe hired a man to help dig into the mound. After working for some time, they unearthed a large rock pile. After pulling off the rocks, they discovered mule bones. Joe and Alvin concluded that the mule must have died while plowing the field and that because of the weight of the animal, the farmer left it where it died and covered it with the rocks and dirt.

With the war looming, in December 1941, Joe and Alvin decided to stop all excavation. However, there was one more place they wanted to explore before they stopped. Their second site of interest was in the area that we now call Merrimac Shores. They were so curious that, while still racing to unearth artifacts at the original site, they took time to dig test sites with their sounding rod throughout this area. These yielded more finds and supported their conclusion that this area was loaded with artifacts. Joe and Alvin mapped the locations of their discoveries and then stopped for the duration of the war, with hopes of picking up after it was over.

In 1945, Joe and Alvin resumed their excavation in the new site they had found before the war. The brothers soon learned that the second site had been sold to developers for a new housing project. This news prompted Alvin and Joe to begin looking for artifacts in this area. In a short time, they found numerous middens that held hundreds of artifacts. Again, just as with the first site, the clock was ticking. The brothers asked for public assistance to support the excavation of the area, but again public interest could not be obtained. As a last resort, they wrote a letter to Mr. Homer L. Ferguson, president of the Mariners' Museum, outlining what they had found at the first site and what they had found up to this point at the second. Mr. Ferguson was very impressed with the findings and agreed that the museum would support excavation of the new site.

With this connection, Alvin and Joe, along with help of the Mariners' Museum, used procedures that were set by the National Parks Service for archaeological research. With these procedures, the site was mapped and catalogued for future research. The teams from the Mariners' Museum

Excavation of the 1945 site. *Courtesy of Virginia Department of Historic Resources.*

were able to unearth artifacts and map the area before construction began on roads and houses. With hundreds of artifacts unearthed at both sites, including the mix of early colonial and Indian artifacts, the Brittinghams concluded that, without a doubt, they had uncovered the Indian village of Kicotan. However, most scholars of the time concluded that the area known as Strawberry Banks, near Hampton University, had been the location of the Kicotan village in the early seventeenth century.

Joe and Alvin were both big believers in sharing this story with others and preserving it for future generations. They would tell the story to anyone who would listen, speaking to church groups and other clubs in the area that had an interest. In 1946, Joe moved his family to Atlanta, Georgia, for a new job. While working there, he would tell stories of his discoveries. His secretary, who was enthralled by these stories, asked Joe to put them to paper. One afternoon, Joe agreed, and in no time his secretary had typed up "The First Trading Post at Kicotan." In 1948, with the story now written, Joe contacted a Newport News printer. Joe's book, which included photographs taken by the Mariners' Museum and a detailed map of the area, was published, and the Brittinghams' story was saved for generations to come.

But the story of the Brittinghams' dig doesn't end with Joe's book. In April 1950, the Smithsonian Institution contacted the brothers and requested to take a look at their collection. After that visit, the brothers decided that their artifacts should be part of the museum's seventeenth- and eighteenth-century collections. In May of that same year, all four-hundred-plus items were gifted to the Smithsonian Institution with the agreement that the collection was to be donated in its entirety, with nothing left behind. The brothers agreed to this, which left them nothing to share with future generations of their families. They felt this was for the best, however, as their collection would be preserved as a whole from which others could learn.

In June 1951, an exhibit of the Brittingham artifacts went on public display. Newspapers from around the country reported on the collection, describing it as being from the earliest American settlement. The Brittingham exhibit was on display for a few months. After it was taken down, the museum used some of the artifacts for other exhibits.

Throughout the years that the Brittinghams' collection has been at the Smithsonian, many scholars in the field of seventeenth-century artifacts have worked on interpreting what the brothers found.

A reassessment of these artifacts undertaken by Nicholas M. Lucceketti of the James River Institute for Archaeological Research and Beverly A. Straube of Jamestown Rediscovery provides significant insight. Their findings indicate that the Brittingham site dates to the first or second quarter of the seventeenth century and might be one of the earliest sites established between Virginia Company lands at Kicotan (east side of Hampton River) and Jamestown. The identification of domestic artifacts in association with a brick chimney base seriously challenges the notion advanced by the Brittinghams that the site was the location of "the first trading post at Kecoughtan." Not only is there no documentary evidence to buttress their claim, but the artifactual evidence strongly suggests another interpretation. Luccketti and Straube noted the presence of high-status domestic items—spurs, bridle ornaments, a sword hilt, firearm components, buckles, furniture hardware, lead musket balls, eating utensils and imported German and Dutch ceramics—which were unlikely to have been traded formally with indigenous peoples and were probably associated with the home of a gentleman. Rather than a trading post, it is more likely that what the Brittingham brothers dug into were the remains of a circa 1625 fortified gentleman's home. In their zeal to uncover the past, the Brittinghams most likely mixed artifacts from earlier

Native American occupations with that of the first Anglo settlements and incorrectly interpreted the site as a "trading post."

Today, the relics unearthed by Joe and Alvin Brittingham remain at the Smithsonian Institute. The Hampton History Museum has been working with the museum to bring some or all of the artifacts home to Hampton to be put on permanent display.

Chapter 4

THE BRITISH LANDING IN WYTHE
AND THE SACK OF HAMPTON

On February 4, 1813, British warships sailed through the Virginia Capes and anchored in Lynnhaven Bay. The war that was declared in June 1812 had at last come to Virginia shores. Shortly after arriving, the British established a naval blockade of the Chesapeake Bay at the Virginia Capes and commenced to seize or destroy as much as possible of the commercial shipping in the Hampton Roads area. A month later, Rear Admiral Sir George Cockburn arrived with additional ships to further strengthen the blockade and to intensify raids and depredations throughout the Chesapeake Bay.

This constant campaign of raiding, seizing ships and attacking coastal fortifications in the bay area would continue for the next two years until the war's end in February 1815. In addition to carrying out naval raids, Cockburn's orders from his superior, Vice Admiral John B. Warren, commander of all British naval forces in North American waters, included the capture of the American frigate USS *Constellation* and, if possible, the port of Norfolk. By the end of April, Cockburn concluded that with his available forces, he would be unable to capture the American frigate or Norfolk. While he waited for additional reinforcements from Admiral Warren, Cockburn left Hampton Roads to conduct more raids in the upper Chesapeake Bay, chiefly along Maryland's Northern and Eastern Shore counties. There, he established a reputation for ruthlessness by conducting such raids according to his own definition of "civilized" warfare.

When Vice Admiral Warren arrived in early June with additional ships and men, the two admirals thought they had sufficient forces for an assault

Left: Admiral Sir George Cockburn. *Courtesy of Hampton History Museum.*

Opposite: Lieutenant Colonel Charles Napier. *Courtesy of Hampton History Museum.*

on Norfolk. On June 22, 1813, British naval and land units under the command of Vice Admiral Warren attempted to take Craney Island at the mouth of the Elizabeth River as a prelude to seizing Norfolk and the American frigate *Constellation*. Approximately 3,500 British troops took part in the Craney Island campaign. The attack consisted of two separate assaults, one by land, commanded by Colonel Sidney Beckwith, and the other by sea, commanded by Captain Samuel Pechell, the admiral's son-

in-law. Assigned to Beckwith's command was the 102nd Infantry Regiment, commanded by Lieutenant Colonel Charles Napier, and approximately 300 soldiers of two independent companies of foreigners. These units were composed mostly of French prisoners of war who had volunteered to fight in North America alongside British forces as a condition for their being released from POW camps in Britain. Royal Marines under the command of Lieutenant Colonel Richard Williams completed the assault force. Captain Pechell's assault force included approximately 1,500 sailors and Royal Marines.

Defending Craney Island was a disparate group of regular militia and sailors and marines from the *Constellation* numbering no more than eight hundred and commanded by Lieutenant Colonel Henry Beatty of the Fourth Virginia Militia. Two companies of Virginia militia artillery—Captain Arthur Emmerson's Portsmouth Light Artillery and Captain James Richardson's Charlotte County artillery—formed the main artillery defenses on the island, assisted by guns and men from the *Constellation*. Commanding the entire militia and regular army units in the Norfolk area and responsible for its overall defense was Brigadier General Robert B. Taylor. By noon on June 22, 1813, the Battle for Craney Island was over and the British assault soundly repulsed, thanks in large part to the withering artillery fire of the Virginia artillery units and the *Constellation*'s guns on both columns of the British assault. British losses, however, were relatively insignificant, with approximately sixteen killed and wounded and another thirty or so missing, mostly deserters from the independent companies. The island's defenders suffered only one casualty, and that was due to an accidental explosion of a gunpowder magazine. By the end of the day, British army and navy units were safely back on their ships, then anchored north of Craney Island. The British troops had suffered a humiliating defeat, and General Taylor did not expect them to withdraw anytime soon. He did, however, expect them to attempt another invasion somewhere in Hampton Roads, and in this belief, he was correct.

Although the *Norfolk Herald* predicted correctly where the next blow would fall, it, unfortunately, was not as accurate in predicting its outcome. It told its readers that "the enemy intends an attack at some other place…it is highly probable they will make an attempt at Hampton…they need not promise themselves that they will be successful. Hampton is well defended." General Taylor knew all too well that Hampton was lightly defended, as he had been informed by Hampton's commander, Major Stapleton Crutchfield, that the town had no more than 450 men for its defense. Crutchfield's detachment consisted of local units from Elizabeth City, York and James City militias, as well as three companies assigned there from Orange and Culpeper Counties. Crutchfield, recognizing that he did, indeed, have only a small force to defend Hampton, nevertheless stoutly stated his intention to Taylor that he would defend the town should the British strike there and would "not abandon or surrender the Post, but in the last moment of a desperate extremity." Crutchfield would soon be tested on that promise.

Hampton, Virginia, circa 1800. *Courtesy of Hampton History Museum.*

Indian River Creek, 2014. *Courtesy of Kelly Siegel.*

Admiral Warren explained to the admiralty that his reason for attacking the small town of Hampton was that it was a center for organizing and collecting militia units from throughout the region and posed a threat to British operations in Hampton Roads. In reality, Hampton possessed no strategic or tactical value to his forces. Norfolk remained the chief British objective, and taking Hampton would not help achieve that goal. Most likely, Warren believed that by taking Hampton, he would provide his forces with a much sought-after victory. The move would also get his men off their ships for a period of respite on dry land. Whatever his reasons, Warren would assign Admiral Cockburn the overall command of the invasion force. As in his Maryland expeditions, Admiral Cockburn would lead the expeditionary force in person and then coordinate with Colonel Beckwith's military forces once on land.

Undoubtedly, Cockburn had at his disposal some charts or maps of Hampton Roads that would enable him to determine the best site for an invasion. He settled on the small inlet of Indian Creek, about two miles west of the town, as the most suitable landing site.

Approximately the same units and companies that had been used to take Craney Island were also to be used for the Hampton assault. Likewise, a naval contingent consisting of upward of forty barges under the supervision of Captain Pechell was sent to the mouth of Hampton Creek and was to act as a feint to cover the major landing force to the west. Several days before the early morning attack on Hampton, Pechell and a small force approached the mouth of Hampton Creek to reconnoiter the town's defenses and, in doing so, drew the artillery fire of the defenses along the creek. By provoking fire, the British knew where the Americans had set up the town's defenses along the creek, and they planned their attack accordingly.

In the early morning hours of June 25, around 4:00 a.m., British forces landed at Indian Creek "in rather more confusion than on the 22nd," recalled Colonel Napier. The landing site would have put the advancing British columns at farmer Murphy's farmhouse and moving up the creek with their boats as far as they could go. Along with Napier's 102nd, were the two independent companies, three companies of Royal Marines, the Royal Marine battalions under Colonel Williams and two six-pounder guns from the Royal Marine Artillery.

Leaving the creek behind, British forces probably marched along a small trail leading northeastwardly through an area of Hampton now known as Olde Wythe until it merged into what was then known as Celey Plantation Road, which led to town from Celey Plantation, about four miles west of Hampton. For the most part, Celey Road roughly followed what is now Shell

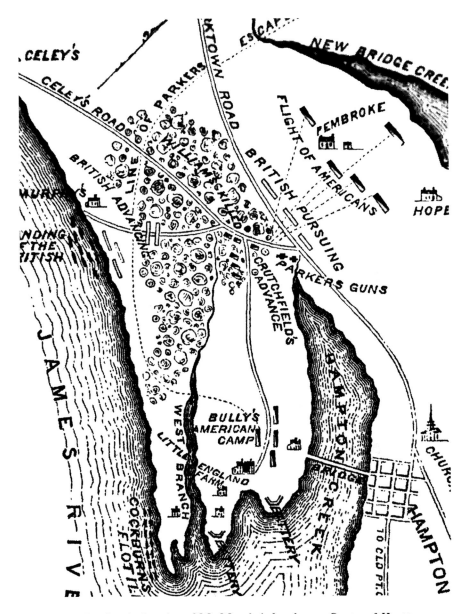

Period map showing the location of Mr. Murphy's farmhouse. *Courtesy of Hampton History Museum.*

Road into west downtown Hampton. Today, Old Celey Road represents the approximate location of the road where it would have intersected the Main Road or Queen Street.

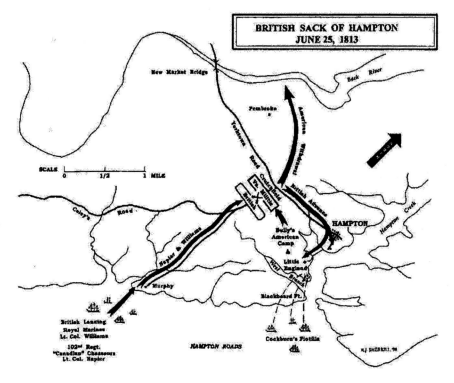

Map portraying the British advance on Hampton. *Courtesy of Hampton History Museum.*

While Beckwith's forces were moving on to Hampton from the west, Pechell's barges began firing some Congreve rockets from just behind Blackbeard's Point. They were aimed at the main military post located at Little England Plantation, between what is now Sunset Creek and the small inlet just west of King Street. According to Major Crutchfield, the British also fired some twelve- and eighteen-pound shot into the camp. At nearby Cedar Point, the militia established a battery of four long twelve-pounder guns. Other guns were situated at the end of King Street. Captain Brazure W. Pryor of the local artillery began to return fire. Major Crutchfield was puzzled by the failure of the British barges to land troops and realized that the display of force in front of him was just a diversion from the main blow. At this time, his patrols along the beachfront had reported to him that a sizeable enemy deployment was advancing along Celey Plantation Road near its juncture with Main Road (Queen Street). Crutchfield quickly gathered most of his militia and marched westward out of town to meet the oncoming foe "to prevent his making an attack on our rear...to surround and cut us off from retreat." Leaving his artillery batteries in place, he advanced to meet the enemy's superior forces with what riflemen and infantry was available to him.

The advance of British troops from the west became more obvious to Crutchfield when a French officer deserted and reported the advance of the enemy. Crutchfield's force entered into a cornfield just west of where Celey Road (Shell) and Main Road (Queen) intersected. It was here, where they first met the enemy's forces driving east, that they "were fired upon by the enemy's musketry from a thick wood of the upper end of a field immediately bordering on the road." The Virginians wheeled about and marched about fifty yards when the enemy opened up with a six-pound field piece along with grape and canister. Crutchfield tried to regroup and get his men into the woods now occupied by Captain Richard Servant's riflemen, "who, with his brave soldiers," Crutchfield recalled later, "acted in a manner of veterans." As Crutchfield's men were getting to the woods, Captain John B. Cooper's cavalry charged the enemy's left flank and was nearly cut off in the process but escaped unharmed. After Captain Servant's riflemen unleashed a volley of well-directed fire toward the enemy, the British opened up with a terrific volley of small arms and cannon that threw the Virginians into brief confusion. During the renewed British fire, Major Gawin Corbin, Crutchfield's second in command, received serious wounds to his left arm and leg while leading his men on horseback. Under pressure from superior enemy forces, Crutchfield organized his men for a hasty retreat. The major later informed General Taylor, "It was indispensably necessary for all our troops to retire, which they did under a continued but ill directed fire from the enemy, who pursued us for two miles with little loss on our part while our men, occasionally stopping at a fence or ditch at every chance, brought down one of the pursuing foe." Most likely, Crutchfield's little band made its escape up what is now Armistead Avenue and across Newmarket Creek. The remnant of Crutchfield's command finally made camp at the Halfway House, approximately six miles to the north of Hampton and the present-day location of the small town of Tabb in York County.

Meanwhile, Captain Brazure W. Pryor's artillery unit along with lieutenants Lively and Jones remained at their batteries and resisted the approaching enemy barges. Lieutenant Lively ordered his men to open fire at the barges when they came within sixty yards. Pryor continued to do so at his location closer to town. When all resistance proved futile and capture appeared imminent, the Virginians spiked their guns and somehow managed to elude the enemy by swimming across the Sunset Creek and escaping to the west. As most of the men were locals, they knew the county and probably made their way back to their homes by evening.

Westwood House. *Courtesy of Hampton History Museum.*

The remains of Mr. Murphy's farmhouse. *Courtesy of Hampton History Museum.*

"I have to perform the painful duty," Major Crutchfield began his initial report to General Taylor, "of apprizing [*sic*] you of my retreat with the garrison under my command at Hampton." Crutchfield reported that his force had sustained 7 killed, 12 wounded, 1 taken prisoner and 11 missing. He estimated that the British had at least 2,500 men but had lost about 200 in the conflict. Two days after the invasion, Beckwith reported to Admiral Warren that his force had suffered 5 killed, 33 wounded and 10 missing. As soon as the American militia was driven out and the town secured, Colonel Beckwith and Admiral Cockburn seized the Westwood House, located one hundred feet from the King Street wharves, as their temporary headquarters.

They would remain there until June 27, when the British started withdrawing their forces from the occupied town. In taking the town, the enemy also seized four twelve-pounder and three six-pounder guns, as well as ammunition and wagons, irreplaceable losses for the Virginia militia. In addition, the British forces seized the militia colors from Captain Jennings's Fauquier militia and from one James City militia light company. Beckwith strategically stationed detachments at outposts guarding the Back River approaches to the town and along the main roads coming into town. The Royal Marines seized St. John's Church as their headquarters and, in the process, ransacked the church and turned its grounds into an outdoor kitchen to slaughter cattle rounded up during the capture.

The full picture of the disastrous results of the British occupation of Hampton would not be known to persons outside of the town for at least a week. Writing his full report to General Taylor from the Halfway House on the twenty-eighth, Major Crutchfield touched on the alleged barbarous behavior of the British occupying forces toward the town's citizens, especially its female population. While many citizens had fled the town just before the enemy's main force entered, enough remained to guard their private property and report their observations. Those who had escaped to neighbors outside town also became subject to British supervision when the enemy posted units to defend against any counterattack.

Captain John B. Cooper of the local militia was among the first officers to enter the city after the British withdrawal. He reported to Crutchfield that the enemy had lost all sense of discipline and decorum in allowing the town to be wantonly ransacked. He described the invading foe as "infamous scoundrels, monsters, destroyed every thing but the houses, and (my pen is almost unwilling to describe it) the women were ravished by the abandoned ruffians." He reported the murder of a Mr. Kirby, who was lying on his deathbed, and the wounding of his wife. Free and enslaved blacks were not only allowed but also encouraged by the invaders to wander around and freely rob persons and houses of all that could be carried away.

Two Norfolk doctors, Dr. John T. Barraud and Dr. William Grayson, requested and received permission from Admiral Warren to cross over to Hampton to render medical care to wounded militia and to any remaining British soldiers left behind. After some delay, they were allowed to enter the still-occupied town on June 26. There, they met Dr. Samuel Colton, a Hampton physician who showed them around the fallen town. The doctors observed the scene of desolation that Cooper had described. From remaining citizens, they learned "that private property in every instance fell a sacrifice to the unlimited ravages of the soldiery. Men of most respectability were pillaged in every respect...were stripped of even the cloathing [sic] which decency renders necessary." They also encountered repeated tales of indecent behavior toward the town's remaining females, some of whom were even seized and sexually violated. Two women would have been violated on the spot had not Colonel Beckwith, himself, intervened to prevent it.

Major Crutchfield also dispatched former assembly delegate Thomas Griffin and current delegate Robert Lively to obtain from Admiral Warren permission to bring needed medical supplies and establish prisoner of war exchanges. On July 2, they landed in Hampton and met with Doctor Colton. They also saw and heard of similar tales of abuse and wanton violation of the town's citizens, especially toward women. After hearing from sources they found too credible to doubt, they noted that "we are compelled to believe that acts of violence have been perpetrated which have disgraced the age in which we live."

By early July, sensational reports of the British occupation of Hampton had slowly made their way into private letters and even the newspapers, such as the *Richmond Enquirer* and *Norfolk Herald*. Barbarous behavior of the sort described in these reports seemed almost too sensational to believe. Resolved to determine if the stories were true, Lieutenant Colonel Richard Parker of the Westmoreland County militia traveled to Hampton to conduct his own fact-finding mission. He found upon approaching the town that the adjacent countryside was indiscriminately plundered with hardly a knife, fork or plate left in the houses. Houses and trunks in town were broken into and every item of conceivable value stolen. The communion plate and service were stolen from the church, and sails from nearby windmills were taken. He confirmed the murder of poor Mr. Kirby and the outrageous tales of the enemy's treatment of the town's females. Parker concluded that the real extent of such violations would never be known, as most women would not come forth due to shame.

However, not all witnesses to the British occupation of Hampton believed the tales of outrage and barbarity to be true. Hancock Lee of Fauquier County was visiting his son in Hampton when the attack occurred. While helping to defend the town, he was taken prisoner aboard a British ship but released shortly thereafter. Hancock later wrote his account of the battle and its aftermath but reported that he was unable to substantiate any of the sensational charges of rape and violations. According to the *Virginia Patriot*, a Federalist newspaper in Richmond and one opposed to the war, Hancock visited almost every house in Hampton and "to our utter astonishment, he states that the accounts of we have received of the savage conduct of the enemy, the abuse of females &c are utterly unfounded." Hancock's account in the *Patriot* was picked up by many of the Federalist prints of the time and republished to sow doubt and to question the more sensational charges published by pro-war newspapers in Virginia and elsewhere. Supporting Hancock's supposition, but not published in newspapers, was the belief of Captain Robert Anderson of the James City militia that there had not been widespread abuse and violation by the enemy at Hampton. Anderson had strong credentials; after all, he was a participant in the battle and was nearly killed for his efforts. To his good friend John Prentis in the Eastern Shore, Anderson later wrote, "I do not believe that a single female was ravished against her own consent by any one of the invading army."

A common thread throughout the eyewitness recollections of the British occupation of Hampton was the recurring charge that the French soldiers in the employ of the British forces were the chief perpetrators of the outrages. There were, at most, three hundred of these soldiers organized into two companies. While most of these soldiers were French, there were also some Germans and Dutch in the ranks. They were taken prisoner during General Wellington's Peninsular Campaign in Spain and agreed to fight with the British in North America as a condition for their being released. In 1813, the British were still very much occupied with Napoleon's army and agreed to use the foreigners because they could spare so few British regiments to North America. The brutal conditions under which the Peninsular Campaign was fought by both sides were well known by Americans at that time. The French mode of warfare separated them from their British comrades in that they were more likely to commit indiscriminate destruction, murder and rape when the opportunity presented itself. Some of the British leaders, such as Colonel Napier of the 102nd, saw the Americans as almost fellow countrymen since they spoke the same language and came from the same culture. "It is quite shocking," he wrote, "to have men who speak our own language brought in wounded; one feels as if they were English peasants and that we were killing our own people." Moreover, many of the French soldiers deeply resented the Virginia militia, whom they charged with shooting down their men in the act of surrendering during the attempt on Craney Island. Eyewitnesses were extremely confident that the perpetrators were French, as the French soldiers could easily be identified since they wore dark green uniforms as opposed to the red and white of the British.

The compelling stories of the outrages and the large number of eyewitness accounts left little doubt in the minds of most Virginians and their political leaders that something truly awful had followed in the wake of the British occupation of Hampton. Major Crutchfield and others had forwarded their accounts to Governor James Barbour, who was incensed by the outrageous tales of abuse and avarice. He ordered Crutchfield and others to gather affidavits from witnesses so that the state could better document the crimes and present them to the British naval commanders for an explanation. Many of the statements made by witnesses about the British occupation of Hampton were included in testimony as part of the investigations made by the U.S. Congress into the charges of British atrocities during the war.

But General Taylor had already acted on his own to demand a satisfactory explanation from the British admirals about the brutal occupation of Hampton. General Taylor dispatched his aide-de-camp, Captain John Myers, to demand that the British explain their actions before Hampton and secure from them a promise that such warfare would not happen again. Admirals Warren and Cockburn claimed that they were not aware of allegations of rape and abuse but referred Myers to Colonel Beckwith, who was in command of the land forces. Beckwith was an experienced professional soldier and, for the times, a humane one. He previously had grave reservations about the use of the French soldiers in the Chesapeake and had written about French insubordination and near mutiny on their way to America. To Myers's question about the killing of Mr. Kirby, Beckwith admitted British cupidity, but as events proved, it was an accidental act and not premeditated. The best Myers could obtain from Beckwith about the British occupation of Hampton was that there had been serious depredations and wanton destruction of the town. Most likely the French troops were responsible, but Beckwith admitted no wholesale rape and physical violations of the women of the town. He advanced the defense that the French soldiers were so incensed about being shot at during the act of surrendering that they wreaked as much havoc on the Virginians as they could. Myers repudiated that explanation as General Taylor had already set up a court of inquiry to look into the charge, and a board of three experienced officers had returned the verdict that there was no credible evidence to support it. Colonel Napier vehemently denied that any of his troops from the 102nd were engaged in any of the alleged acts. Napier thought the idea of using the French troops was an accident waiting to happen, and he was happy to see that Beckwith was sending the French soldiers away to Canada as soon as he could procure ships. The French, Napier believed, "were the greatest rascals existing. Much I wanted to shoot some, but had no opportunity." Cockburn's aide-de-camp, Lieutenant James Scott, scoffed at the idea of wholesale rape and murder, but he also thought that whatever outrages had been perpetrated at Hampton were caused by the French soldiers.

The British evacuated the town of Hampton beginning on June 27, but their forces remained in the vicinity for nearly five days, bivouacking along the beach from Old Point Comfort to what is now Buckroe Beach. They, no doubt, occupied the old lighthouse at the Point for observation purposes. Beckwith urged Admiral Warren to remove his troops by the beginning of July in fear that enough Virginia militia could be assembled to threaten his forces. By July 3, some of Warren's ships under the command of Admiral Cockburn were on their way to Ocracoke, North Carolina, to raid that coast and seize ships. Others remained on blockade duty, while still others sailed up the James as far as Charles City County raiding shores and seizing commercial ships. In Richmond, a brief panic occurred in July, caused by fears that the British were on their way up the James to do to the capital city what they had done in Hampton.

Whatever the nature of the purported outrages against the citizens of Hampton on June 25, 1813, the full extent will likely never be fully known. That something despicable and degrading occurred appears to be in little doubt, but was it wholesale rape and murder? It seems unlikely that wholesale rape or murder accurately describes what happened at Hampton. Were women violated in a sexual sense? Perhaps. The term "violation" as it was used in the early nineteenth century could also refer to the placing of hands on a woman's body during an attempt to steal a ring or other jewelry. Only one "murder" was documented, and that description later proved to be inaccurate, as Mr. Kirby's widow many years later informed Mr. Benson Lossing, the author of the *Field Book of the War of 1812* (1857), that British soldiers were shooting at their dog when they hit poor Mr. Kirby and wounded him. Certainly, wanton destruction and theft of innocent citizens of Hampton occurred. Hampton's citizens probably suffered more severely from the British occupation of their town than any other during the war. Virginians at the time did not know it, but the incident at Hampton would be the last time that British forces would occupy any part of Tidewater Virginia.

After Hampton, Virginians would also have a new array of heroes to add to their already impressive list from other wars. Men like Major Stapleton Crutchfield, Major Gawin Corbin, Captain Brazure W. Pryor, Captain Richard Servant and Captain John B Cooper would be held up to Virginians as examples of courage and bravery. Unfortunately, their names have been all but lost to history. Hampton itself would also become a symbol for revenge and of the type of warfare that the British were willing to wage in this Second War of Independence.

Chapter 5

SCHOOLS CALLED WYTHE

From 1909 to 2010, students from the Wythe neighborhood attended schools located on the corner of Claremont Avenue and Kecoughtan Road that carried the name of George Wythe.

The first Wythe School opened in March 1909 with approximately 125 students. Elizabeth City County school superintendent John Willis named the new building the George Wythe School in honor of the first chancellor of Virginia. The school was built for the growing population of children who were attending two smaller, overcrowded schools in the area. This new school came to fruition through the collaborative efforts of the school system and the Wythe Protective Service, a civic group that worked on various issues within the Wythe area.

The school's cornerstone, a gift from the local Tammany Lodge, whose members were great supporters of education, was laid on Thanksgiving morning, 1908. In celebration, a ceremony to showcase the plans for the construction of the new, modern school building was held to coincide with the Virginia Teacher's Association Conference being held in Newport News. The state superintendent of public instruction, the Honorable J.D. Eggleston, gave the keynote address at the celebration. In addition to the conference attendees, a large number of residents and children attended the ceremony to hear speeches on education.

The two-story building cost a total of $11,000. This included $1,500 for the lot and $9,000 for the building. The remaining $500 was used to purchase equipment for the school. The school was built with four classrooms, each with a capacity of fifty students, and a principal's office. Two of the four classrooms were left unfinished to save on costs. The basement held playrooms and the heating plant. The school was designed so that additions could be easily built to double or quadruple its size. The first principal was Miss Rosa Dexter, and Miss Grace Thornton and Miss Nettie Montgomery were the first teachers. The school opened without a United States flag to hoist. This was remedied when the local chapter of the Junior Order of United American Mechanics presented a flag to the school during a ceremony held in October 1909.

A few months after the school opened, the Wythe Protective Service was already putting pressure on the school superintendent to have those unfinished classrooms completed, as overcrowding had quickly become a pressing issue. The first addition was completed in 1912. A $12,000 bond was issued and was bought by a local Hampton investor named Hamoden Mugler. Over two hundred students were enrolled at that time, and with increasing numbers of families moving into the area, more classroom space was needed.

In 1919, a vote on a bond issue to fund a new school was defeated. But in June 1920, another bond issue, this one for money to build an addition to the school, was voted on and passed. This new addition was called the "Annex" by the students and held classrooms for the primary grades along with a library and an assembly hall used for student programs and presentations and which also served as a place for community meetings.

By the early 1930s, the student population had reached over six hundred students, two hundred over the building's capacity. Overcrowding was so bad that the school turned two smaller rooms, including one in the basement that was used for storage, into classrooms. The school also was allowed to use two upstairs rooms of the Perkins Grocery Store, located on Claremont Avenue, and a nearby building on Kecoughtan Road to hold additional classrooms. Other means to curb overcrowding included having two start times for the primary grades, one at 8:30 a.m. and the other at 11:30 a.m., and a half-year school calendar, which was used to promote students to the next grade faster.

In 1935, the Wythe Protective Service again stepped in to lead the efforts to add more classrooms to the building. The school district took action and explored two options—adding more classrooms to the current building or building a new school. It eventually chose to build a new school. After looking at a few sites throughout the area, plans were made to build a junior high school on the land adjoining the school where the Perkins Grocery Store stood. This new school, named Wythe Junior High School, would serve students in seventh, eighth and ninth grades.

A 1920 picture of the George Wythe School showing the third addition. *Courtesy of Jackie Potter.*

In December 1936, a groundbreaking ceremony was held for the new junior high school. Construction costs included $155,000 for the school building and an additional $30,000 for equipment and supplies. An $81,000 grant from the federal government helped cover some of the expenses, with the balance of $100,000 coming from a bond issue passed through a vote by citizens. Upon completion of this building, two hundred students would move from the Wythe School, giving the crowded primary grades more space.

The school system and community hoped to have the building finished in time for the September opening of the 1937–38 school year. Unfortunately, the weather did not cooperate, and a bitter winter slowed down construction. The school year started after Labor Day, but the new junior high building did not open until the end of October.

The three-story, T-shaped building could accommodate five hundred students and had all the latest in modern conveniences of the day, including fireproofing and opaque Pyrex glass sections that allowed in light. The school was also designed with a heating system that could heat the existing building and up to ten additional classrooms if the need for expansion arose in the future. The first floor housed three classrooms; two industrial arts shops, which the school board hoped to use for night classes to provide

71

The mascot patch worn by Wythe School students during the 1940s to demonstrate pride in their school. *Courtesy of Greg Siegel.*

unemployed youth with job-finding skills; supply rooms; and a boiler room. Six classrooms, girls' and boys' locker rooms and showers, the auditorium and the gymnasium were on the second floor, and on the top floor were two classrooms and several science rooms.

In the 1920s, the owl was chosen as the Wythe School's mascot. In a 2010 interview, Doris Smith, who attended the George Wythe School, remembered a Wythe School cheer: "Wise old owl…Hoot, hoot, hoot!" She also remembered a phrase that was common to the students: "The less we spoke, the more we heard. Let us be like that wise old bird."

One of the unique features of the school was the placement of the school's mascot, the owl, over the two front doors. Another unique feature was the following saying engraved above the entrance door: "Enter to learn. Leave to serve." This saying is attributed to St. John Baptist de La Salle, a French priest who was passionate about education. Beginning in the 1880s, LaSalle

Institutes were opened throughout the United States by the Brothers of the Christian Schools, and many are still operating in cities across America today. In 1898, a group of Brothers founded the LaSalle Institute for Boys on the corner of LaSalle Avenue and Chesapeake Avenue. The school closed in 1904, and the building went though various incarnations. It was a hotel called the Boulevard Inn until 1914, at which point it became a rooming house for families of soldiers stationed in the area. Finally, it was transformed into a six-unit apartment building. The building was torn down in 1987 to make way for the condominiums we see today.

Parents and community members were part of the Wythe School's history from the beginning. Today, this group is known as the PTA; however, back in 1909, the group was known as the Patrons League. The group's mission in 1909, as it continues to be today, was to support the school and its teachers in bringing the best education possible to the students. The Patrons League undertook its first project a few days before the school opened, when volunteers helped to remove construction materials and spruced up the grounds by planting shrubs and trees. During the first year, the group also raised money to buy equipment for the school, such as maps, globes, reference books and other learning materials, by holding dinners in the community.

The Patrons League grew along with the school. It staffed a small library in the school, offering books that had been donated or bought by the organization, and raised the necessary funds to pay for the first playground equipment. The group also opened a small lunchroom in the basement of the Annex, even though most children "brown-bagged it" or walked home for lunch. The Patrons League hired one worker and, along with help from volunteers, made soup, peanut butter and jelly sandwiches and other items available for sale to the students. When students did not have the few cents needed to buy lunch, the Patrons League gave them lunches for free. When the junior high school was built, the group operated in both schools as one organization, supporting the growing populations of both schools.

During the summer of 1939, the county organized the first summer recreation activities held at the school's playground. During the opening week, it was reported that over one thousand children attended. For the boys, some of the available activities included hand tennis, ping-pong, checkers and an organized baseball team, with games played against playground teams from Newport News for "bragging rights." For the girls, there were craft classes that taught them how to weave and how to make hand puppets, scrapbooks and other crafts. The school library was open in the mornings so that children could check out books for summer reading, and a class for those needing extra help in reading was held each day. The summer programs continued for years and were something the children of Wythe looked forward to each summer.

By the end of the 1940s, it was determined that the 1909 school building, now called George Wythe Elementary School, had outlived its time. A new George Wythe Junior High School was built on Catalpa Avenue and opened for the 1950–51 school year. This school was known to have the most modern features of the time and was even featured in a national magazine. It also featured artwork by local artist Jack Clifton, a nationally and internationally renowned artist, teacher and author. Mr. Clifton's stone carvings with the words "Learn to Live" and "Live to Learn" adorned the front entrance of the school. The quote is attributed to Bayard Taylor, an American poet during the 1800s. The line is from a poem to his daughter called "Learning." The elementary school students were relocated to the old junior high school, and the building was renamed George Wythe Elementary School. The owl was used as the mascot of both this school and the new junior high school.

The original George Wythe School laid vacant until 1957, when a group of Wythe citizens approached the school board and proposed to have the land turned into a neighborhood pool and tennis courts. The George Wythe Recreation Association was organized. The old school was torn down in 1959. The city instructed the demolition company to leave the basement open for the beginning of the pool in order to keep costs down for the group. Bricks from the fallen building were sold to local neighbors, who in turn used them as filler for low areas on their property. A large fence with barbed wire was erected around the site until the neighborhood pool and tennis courts were completed.

The only time a Wythe School on the corner of Claremont Avenue and Kecoughtan Road did not serve students was during the 1977–78 and 1978–79 school years, when the students were temporarily moved to Sinclair Elementary on Coliseum Drive in order for the Wythe building to undergo major renovations. But the Wythe name did not go away. Sinclair Elementary was renamed Sinclair-Wythe Elementary School for those two years to make the Wythe students feel welcome and a part of their temporary home. During the renovation, the school district held a sale at Wythe School to sell off old equipment, which would be replaced with new, modern equipment. Desks, tables and chairs were sold to anyone who wanted them. Most of these items were sold to former students as keepsakes.

One of artist Jack Clifton's stone interpretations on the front of Wythe Junior High School. *Courtesy of Greg Siegel.*

In 2008, the Hampton City School Board decided to build two new schools within the city. Several years earlier, the land on Victoria Boulevard where the Sentara Hospital stood was left vacant when the hospital moved to a new location. The owners of the hospital sold the land to the City of Hampton for future use. This site was a perfect location for one of the new schools, and the decision was made to close Wythe Elementary at the end of the 2009–10 school year. In June 2010, a large farewell celebration was held on the Wythe Elementary School grounds. Hundreds of the school's former students, teachers, principals and supporters came one last time to walk the halls and visit with old school colleagues and friends. The school history was displayed throughout the building, and former students and staff were asked to bring mementos to share. A ceremony was held with songs, speeches and recognition of former students. The ceremony ended with each former student in attendance ringing a small school bell.

As of the date of this book's publication, the Wythe Elementary School building has been used by Hampton City Schools as a storage building since its closing in 2010, when the new school was opened on Victoria Boulevard. In the spring of 2013, the school board, along with the Hampton Planning Department, began gathering input and ideas for the reuse of the building and/or property. Only time will tell what is in store.

Chapter 6

THE BOULEVARD

The following chapter, taken from John Feye's Hampton Roads and Four Centuries as a World's Seaport *(1996), is reprinted with the kind permission of Edwin Mellen Press. It weaves a delightful story of the past using interviews from people who lived along this charming avenue in the 1990s.*

On the map and street signs it's an avenue, to its people, "The Boulevard," though no flower-bedded parkway serving only mansions. There are those, also modest homes, more.

"The Boulevard," Chesapeake Avenue, runs three miles along the Roadstead shore of Hampton and Newport News, the longest stretch in the two cities (maybe any) with no traffic light. From when it was an Indian path, it has given a vista of history. The Spanish saw it. George Washington knew it as a lovesick young man socializing [and] later sailed past it to talk to Admiral de Grasse about Yorktown. British troops came ashore in the War of 1812. The *Monitor-Virginia* battle was watched from it.

Theodore Roosevelt's Great White Fleet gathered and returned in sight of all. Woodrow Wilson walked and continued to play golf. Warships, transports, tankers and munitions freighters crowded before it in two World Wars. That one day during the seventy-two-day 1981 coal strike, those fifty-nine colliers lay in sight.

"The Boulevard" is the only place to look east past Old Point Comfort and Fort Wool into lower Chesapeake Bay, south to Norfolk and Portsmouth, west to Newport News Point at the mouth of the James River, southwest to

An aerial photograph of the eastern section of Wythe taken from a U.S. Army dirigible in 1927 and showing the Boulevard. *Courtesy of Hampton History Museum.*

The battle of the *Monitor* and *Merrimack* as seen near Wythe shores. *Courtesy of the Mariners' Museum.*

the Nansemond. On clear nights look east again for lights, at least the loom, of Norfolk's Ocean View and Virginia Beach's Chesapeake Bay shores. With a reflecting overcast, twenty-second flashes from the Cape Henry lighthouse show. In season, the sun or full moon rise from and set in water. In calm dawn or dusk, Venus can shoot an arrow the five-mile length. If a navigational star's azimuth is right, you get a natural horizon for sextant practice.

Here, and nowhere else, you see all Hampton Roads.

Norfolk has waterfront, most of it along or near Hampton Roads in industry, commerce, boat yards and marinas, motels, restaurants, and the Navy. Portsmouth sees mostly the Elizabeth River, Chesapeake Dismal Swamp, both scenic, but not broad water. Virginia Beach shores see only the lower Bay and the Atlantic.

"The Boulevard" runs west from Hampton's LaSalle Avenue to Newport News' small Anderson Park and Peterson Boat Basin, once the mouth of Salters Creek. From 1916 to 1927, when it joined Newport News, from the present Hampton line west to Salters Creek was a town of Kecoughtan, then and still "one of the very best residence sections on the Peninsula" though in the late 1980s briefly threatened with a pox of condos or a high-rise by a developer.

"The Boulevard" goes on, as Newport News' Sixteenth Street, away from water through a housing development, to end just east of railway yards, James River coal piers, and Newport News International Terminal piers.

At the Hampton end, a big house at the foot of LaSalle, now replaced by a condominium, was once the Boulevard Inn. Just east Church Creek, named for the Elizabeth City Parish Church first built by it between 1610 and 1620, flowed into the Roads. There, where old Alfred Lavallette lived on a houseboat full of USS *Constitution* and Civil War mementos and raised terrapins until the 1933 hurricane, the creek is mostly just low ground. Kecoughtan, the Indian village, may have been on its bank.

Hampton and Newport News shores of Chesapeake Avenue have changed in our century. "Pioneers" have seen Elizabeth City County farmland become city residential, some elegant. Those who swam off beaches now see almost no beaches, gone in tidal currents and storms. Seawalls and riprap give a little protection against hurricane seas and tides, though even in moderate summer southerlies surf spouts through the riprap in places to eat dirt and grass at high tide. Hurricanes blow shingles off ashore and spray shrubs and windows with salt. Some think shore erosion started with the Hampton Roads Bridge-Tunnel. The long bridge approach to the mile-long tunnel under the channel changed currents, they think. Or the heavy

Before the 1960s, Wythe was noted for its wide sandy beaches. This photograph was taken on the Boulevard between Manteo and Hampton Roads Avenues. *Courtesy of Shirley Sue Wallace.*

shipping of two World Wars. Still others recall beaches getting narrower at least since the 1933 hurricane. Miss Fanny Landon, whose parents, Mr. and Mrs. W.H. Landon, bought a piece of farmland for a home in 1901, when she was three, saw fifty feet or more disappear before she died in 1988. Without the seawall, built in the 1930s by the Works Progress Administration, she felt there now "would be no front yards—or back—nothing."

The erosion concerns Hampton's Chesapeake Avenue residents. They own to the water across "The Boulevard." Newport News' Chesapeake Avenue waterside is city-owned, but in Hampton the people mow grass, get riprap, and pick up trash. If concrete is poured nearby, the transit-mix driver can be asked to dump any leftover in a hole.

Mowing grass is no great chore, the ground mostly level for the double-track trolley line washed away in the 1933 hurricane. But trash, even if no worse than anywhere, can be a damned nuisance to residents keeping the strip neat, as they often must do by picking up after a warm weekend. Hampton streets to "The Boulevard" have public parking on the waterside, and three or four cars, radios loud, can generate plenty. It must delight distilleries, breweries, soft drink peddlers, and pizza, chicken, and fast-food joints to see non-biodegradable evidence of popularity. Occasionally a man goes along with a sack but at a cent for an aluminum can, there are easier ways to get whisky money.

Residents put old utility poles and railroad ties end-to-end close to the pavement to keep cars off the grass. This has been most necessary July Fourth, when crowds watch fireworks in Norfolk or at Fort Monroe. Otherwise you pick up more trash, often fill in where cowboys spin wheels. The last George Smith told one young buck, who actually asked permission, to park but bring a load of topsoil to fill any holes. The fellow drove off. The general situation improved with the city finally posting "Private Property" signs and others forbidding fishing, closing street-end "Scenic Overlooks" at ten p.m., and setting a twenty-five-mile speed limit. Promised "total enforcement" of the speed limit lasted a few weeks.

This is perhaps a price of civilization. Yet people like Fanny Landon and others who lived most of their lives along "The Boulevard" could tell of days when the price seemed reasonable. Miss Landon saw the streetcar line laid down along the shore, the second of two joining Hampton and Newport News. The other ran along Electric Avenue, a mile inland, to become, more elegantly, Victoria Boulevard in 1946 when the tracks were torn up. Until the second line came, "We had to walk a mile to catch a car."

"The cars were two-man, motorman and conductor, and the fare from Newport News was a nickel to Hampton Roads Avenue." That north–south street is almost two blocks west of her family home. "The motorman was supposed to make us get off there or pay another nickel. But sometimes they'd forget and stop at our house. Mother always had coffee for them!" Miss Landon also remembered the carmen in cold weather with a kerosene heater, when power failed and a trolley was stalled near.

Betty Martin, who grew up on the little Indian River, a tributary creek west a few blocks, where British landed in the War of 1812, remembered also that pranking neighborhood boys made the run one of the least liked by the carmen.

"The kids would pile brush and trash on the tracks and sometimes set it afire when they heard the trolley coming behind the curve there," she recalled. "The car had to stop and the motorman and conductor get out and push the fire off the tracks, and the boys ran behind and pulled the trolley pole off the wire.

"Then one time the boys put a big stone block on the track and covered it with brush. They didn't set it afire. The motorman thought he could just push through and his cowcatcher would clear the track. He hit the block and had to stop. His cowcatcher was all bent. He and the conductor had to push the block out of the way before they could go on." These were no Halloween pranks. The carmen could expect them at any time the boys were out of school.

A neighbor a block west of the Landons was Ernest W. Sniffen, an engineer at The Shipyard. His son, Harold, retired assistant director and curator of prints at The Mariners' Museum, recalled that his father built there in 1910 "because that was as far as he could ride for a nickel." He liked the summer southerlies off the water, and gave his house Hiawatha's name for the south wind, Shawondassee. He also like the say if he looked east, the next land was Portugal.

"The Boulevard" served many "Shipyard families," more from the National Advisory Committee for Aeronautics, today's Langley Research Center of the National Aeronautics and Space Administration. Big houses were built, some with gingerbread and towers, several, years later, to rent rooms or apartments as children scattered and old folks found themselves with too much house. In the 1930s the neighborhood became a "little Athens," with dozens of NACA scientists and engineers who came to "The Boulevard" or near. Among them were John Stack, a Collier Trophy winner; H.J.E. Reid, a director; Charles Hastings, founder of an electronic navigation firm; and the late F.L. Thompson, a director. Bill and Betty Martin remember NACA's Eastman Jacobs building an airplane to fly from a neighboring field.

Where young blades now sit in parking areas, drink, smoke pot, and get droopy-glassy over car radios—at least until someone calls police—in Fanny Landon's time there was much to be enjoyed from a front porch.

"On Christmas Eve the harbor was filled with ships, mostly Navy, and all outlined in lights. I think they were battleships with the old basket masts."

Navy officers often came to Hampton, some to live in those big houses. Proper folk in Norfolk put up signs, "No dogs or sailors," but "The Boulevard" welcomed the officers. "The Fergusons [Homer Ferguson, shipyard president] were friends of Mother's and Father's, and when ships were taken in for repair, we met the officers. Once one staying at our house said to us, 'Come on, let's go for a ride.' We didn't have an automobile, so we thought that was wonderful. He was captain of the biggest ship at The Shipyard. It was Raymond Spruance! He was a lieutenant commander. I was only nineteen then. He stayed at our house and went by Navy boat to the Navy Base at Norfolk."

Miss Landon had seen, among great liners that crossed or anchored in Hampton Roads, the *Leviathan* going to or from The Shipyard. "Seeing ships was just as exciting as going to the movies—and we didn't go to the movies often!"

Ernest Sniffen rode the *Leviathan* on her trial run after reconversion from transport. He, and many others, had worked on her. Shipyard workers and others from near and far crowded "The Boulevard" for the *Leviathan*, the *United States*, the *America*, and for great warships. George Smith remembered coming out of the tunnel to see an aircraft carrier, back from overseas, passing the Chamberlin. When he got home, "The Boulevard" was tightly parked.

From her porch, Miss Landon could see the double-ended Norfolk ferry at the end of Manteo Avenue, a few blocks farther west. "It ran all the time, every time he got a chance, unless the weather was too awful. It took about a half-hour to cross. We used to go and watch it come in."

The Landons did not use it. "We always went to Newport News and rode the C. and O. Virginia free. My father was the agent for the Old Dominion Steamboat Line and we had a pass. All the lines and the railroad gave passes then. When I went to school at Fredericksburg, I rode on a pass. Everybody was doing it. Father had a pass on the streetcar line. He gave one to Mother." Harold Sniffen remembers going under the ferry pier to look for coins dropped through cracks. Also spending a find in the pier store for a penny Tootsie Roll, once he learned this roll was not bread. There were big nickel ones, too, if you found a nickel. The Martins also remember swimming off an adjacent pier, with a few youngsters drowning in the deep hole made by the wash.

Another Sniffen boyhood memory is of the presidential yacht's tender coming to the pier, Woodrow Wilson walking with his golf bag a block east, then up to the Hampton Roads Golf Club's now forgotten links, the first in Virginia. One tee was almost at the Sniffen back door.

Another "Boulevard" visitor by yacht was Bud Fisher, whose Mutt and Jeff are better known to many than Woodrow Wilson. Fisher anchored off the Landon home, then a small resort hotel, Widewater, and Mr. Landon rowed him, his wife, and mother-in-law ashore for a few days in a house with "electric lights and long distance telephone." A couple could stay a week for twenty or twenty-five dollars.

Miss Landon was fond of Old Point Comfort's Chamberlin Hotel. "One time we were in the Chamberlin eating and I said, 'Look—there's a submarine!' It was just out the window. It was fascinating—the first time I had seen a submarine come in." Ships do seem to pass just outside the dining room. The Bay is forty to sixty feet deep close inshore, and steamboats stopped at the pier, now gone, until automobiles and trucks made us "mobile."

The disastrous fire of March 7, 1920, was another of Miss Landon's Chamberlin memories. "Grandma's nephew, Mr. [Elliott] Braxton, was at the Chamberlin for dinner. He finished and took the streetcar home and got off at LaSalle Avenue and walked down to the beach. Somebody said, 'Look!' He turned around and said, 'The Chamberlin! On fire!' He was lucky he had gotten out. I thought at first it was the sun reflected from the windows."

(Early March 31, 1985, fire, a mile east of "The Boulevard" and visible from all Hampton Roads, put beyond salvage another Hampton Landmark, the ninety-nine-year-old Strawberry Bank Manor. This was built as Roseland Manor, then sold to Harrison Phoebus, owner of the Hygeia Hotel, the Chamberlin predecessor. Strawberry Bank was the Phoebus home until his widow, Annie, died in 1906. It was an official State Landmark and listed in the

National Register of Historic Places. Before the fire, you could walk along its shore, look back at the Queen Anne chateau, overlook parked cars of a half dozen tenant professional firms, and know a little of our "Gilded Age.")

Hampton Roads seemed clean enough for the Landons and many others along "The Boulevard" to swim, even with sanitary sewers running out from shore. Today you would risk an oil slick, small but messy, spilled or pumped from a bilge to blacken a few square feet of beach or riprap (a trifle compared to what had to be endured during two World Wars.) You would dodge among crabpot floats drifted astray but more plastic jugs, even a hard hat lost overboard, and underfoot broken whisky bottles. And always yellow signs—don't take shellfish! Seeing oysters on today's storm sewer outfalls, or clam shells dropped by gulls to break open on the seawall, you might wish for a gull's digestion. You still would have to contend with an occasional riprap rat, fat on chicken bones, sandwich crusts, and other garbage left in parking areas.

Fanny Landon remembered that the last oyster stake offshore was as far as anybody ought to swim. Harold Sniffen had a memory of three sandbars paralleling the beach, thick eel grass full of crabs in the troughs, the oyster stake beyond the farthest. Boys rowed out to "skinny dip."

"One time I was out on the bar with my two brothers, and I stepped off into deep water," Miss Landon recalled. "One of them looked and saw nothing but bubbles. He came out and got me." Rescue can be needed now. A driver speeding down LaSalle Avenue in a late night alcoholic fog may not turn. Then his car jumps the guard rail. If anybody around is awake, he too can be fished, presumably sober.

As with any through street, "The Boulevard" still gets to be a speedway, drivers taking their God-given right to do fifty in any twenty-five-mile zone. It was closed to through traffic for a few months in 1985 to rebuild a bridge over Indian River. Residents east liked the thinned traffic. Some even urged keeping the bridge for pedestrians and bicycles only. To others in the longer stretch west the thought was "elitism" since speeding continued there almost to the bridge.

Speeding cars and howling radios are two nuisances. All day people from time to time have to stop talking, telephoning, or listening while a military helicopter thumps by, along the shoreline and five hundred feet up if the pilot civilized, overhead or blocks inland and two hundred feet, even tree-top, if still adolescent. Or a jet, circling a half-dozen times to land at the Naval Air Station across the water, coasts under a thousand feet, its engines a stuck calliope. Protests get "There, there" or "Who, us?" responses, plus a two-week neighborhood buzzing. Nothing is heard in City Halls but the rustle of federal dollars.

Miss Landon knew "The Boulevard" and Hampton Roads would go on changing in the more than eighty years she watched them. Change to be remembered included the old Robison brickyard, where "The Boulevard" runs behind a small bulge in the shoreline a half mile west, becoming a tennis court and homes built by J.C. and Tome Robinson for their families in the 1890s, then for others in the neighborhood's first "development." The Wythe community of Elizabeth City County was annexed by Hampton in the early 1950s, when more and more homes came to be.

The Chamberlin, now a National Historic Place against the bureaucratic wish of the Army, legal owner of the real estate, she hoped "would stay there forever." In the bight to the mouth of the Hampton River, in view of Chamberlin windows, "we used to see small boats, fishing boats and others, come in bad weather. It was a most fascinating sight." A northerly blow now sends small boats into Hampton River, but on summer Wednesdays, dozens of sailboats swarm out to cross the bight on the windward leg of the Hampton Yacht Club race course around channel buoys on the Norfolk side.

Small boats today are mostly crabbers', with clam dredges on Hampton Flats. The shoreline is no longer for pleasure boating, the water too shallow for cruising sailboats, too exposed to all but northerly winds. Piers still in use have davits or ramps for their boats. Some sailing people do carry small catamarans and wind-surfers to the water.

Most piers have been removed, partly because no longer safe, more because too many people fish, crab, sun, drink, smoke pot, neck, property owners vulnerable to suits if anybody falls off. "Attractive nuisances," as lawyers have it, never mind your "No Trespassing" signs.

One good pier was found to be the watch station for a housebreaker, who timed goings and comings. He knifed his way out when found in one house. He went to jail, though not for that. Other felonious ventures occasionally have been hinted. Once an outboard launch, with no motor, was anchored for a few days fifty feet out. Hampton police said nobody had reported a boat missing and if nobody's interested we're not. Then a resident recalled seeing, late one night, flashing lights and busy men. So a few bales of marijuana likely were landed, the boat abandoned. Another time an outboard with nobody aboard circled until it ran ashore and burned. Later, cars turned into parking areas, paper sacks were passed one way, envelopes the other, and wheels spun. Older residents remembered flashing lights and mysterious business during Prohibition. Nothing was new.

Thus "The Boulevard" of late. No streetcar again will stop for Miss Landon's coffee, no Landon dog will bring home a live chicken—"Mother would nearly have a fit"—to Fanny Landon's childhood delight. The small Civil War house just west of LaSalle, from which the *Monitor-Virginia* battle was watched and where Civil War photographer Matthew Brady lived for a time, was partly restored from what an interim owner did to "modernize" it. "It looked like they put it in a crate to ship off." Miss Landon wouldn't have been satisfied unless it looked as it did when she was a child. Nobody has to level corn hills, as Ernest Sniffen did more than three-quarters of a century earlier for grass to be cut by a hand-pushed reel mower.

But ducks, geese, and swans still fly over, spring and fall, also purple martins. Swallows nest under pier decks. A few ducks winter along the riprap. A pair of skimmers dip beaks. An occasional sandpiper looks for sand. Herons squawk their way from the Bay to the James. Stingrays and skates school, and people gather to watch wingtips cutting water, noses rooting for clams. A gull may struggle against a turtle holding its legs. Other gulls go crazy over a school of bunkers. A sick fin whale sixty feet long, looking for a quiet place to die, stranded on a bar off "The Boulevard" in late 1987, then wandered off at high tide, bumped a racing sailboat, and tried other Roadstead bars before being "put to sleep mercifully," as we do with old pets, and towed out to sea for Nature's own scavengers. Strangely, shoot-it-if-it-moves sports did not invoke the Second Amendment to use it for target practice, as had happened to a sick whale up the James River at another time.

Ships anchor, voyages completed or to start when holds are full of coal or grain or decks stacked to the bridges with containers. The Navy put a new ammunition pier out in the middle, and it can be hoped nobody sneaks a smoke. Those towers ashore might be blown off.

Along "The Boulevard" residents mow lawns, paint houses, and do yard work according to their years. George Smith told of a neighbor working on his knees on grass along the sidewalk when a big, air-conditioned car with two blue-haired ladies stopped. One lowered a window to ask, "Are you the yard man?"

"I guess I am," he replied.

"What do you change?"

"Well, she's never paid me a cent," he said, "but she lets me sleep with her every night."

So, come by. Get the feeling, as so many did in those "pioneer" days, that "We knew we got to 'The Boulevard' when the air changed." That summer southerly off the water, that Shawondassee that for Hiawatha. Filled the air with dreamy softness. Gave a twinkle to the water. Will do it for you still, if a four o'clock squall isn't thundering from beyond the James.

Chapter 7

THE PENINSULA'S MAIN STREET: KECOUGHTAN ROAD

Kecoughtan Road, one of the main arteries between the cities of Hampton and Newport News, has seen many changes over the last one hundred years. Its heyday was in the 1940s and '50s, when the population of Wythe was increasing rapidly with the growth of industry and the influx of government workers. Spurred by this population growth, developers built the Wythe Plaza, and other smaller plazas sprouted up nearby, adding larger stores, restaurants and service businesses to the existing mix of small stores and gas stations that lined the road since its beginning in 1910.

In 1891, the Old Dominion Land Company mapped out streets on the west side of Wythe, from Salter's Creek to today's Claremont Avenue on the land of the old Celey Plantation. The developers designed streets, including one called Third Street (today's Kecoughtan Road), which ran from the Newport News city line to Catalpa Avenue. Third Street was a dirt road about fifty to sixty feet wide with side streets measuring eighty feet wide or wider running to the harbor to the south and to Shell Avenue to the north.

Walking, horseback riding and horse-drawn wagons were the main modes of transportation at this time. It was not until 1905 or so that increasing numbers of citizens began to own automobiles, which made better roads in the area a necessity. In 1908, after being pressured by local business owners and civic associations, Elizabeth City County officials looked into connecting Third Street with a road that would continue east to Hampton's city line.

In early 1909, the county started the process of planning a road that was being called the "New Store Road." The road would be thirty to fifty feet wide with a six-inch roadbed composed of small stones mixed with a petroleum product that was compacted with a roller; it looked like cement after it dried. The estimated cost of the road was $23,000. The Commonwealth of Virginia's contribution would be only $12,000, paid in equal amounts over a three-year period. The county would add only $5,000, leaving a shortfall of $6,000. The county notified the community that if the new road was to be constructed, help was needed to raise the additional funds. Help came when Frank Darling and W.C. Armstrong, two local business leaders, stepped up to become heads of the funding committee. Soon this committee started calling on businessmen and private citizens to collect funds needed to build the road. In a few months, the remaining $6,000 was raised. Mr. Darling and Mr. Armstrong took an additional step to making the road a reality when they signed personal notes so that the Commonwealth of Virginia's three-year commitment would not stop the contractor from being paid in full once the road was completed.

In November 1909, work began on surveying and staking out New Stone Road. It started at the Salter's Creek Bridge, which lies near Greenlawn Cemetery and was built by the county in 1906. The surveyors followed Third Street and worked their way west, stopping just short of the Jackson Street Bridge (Sunset Creek). The land needed for the road was given to the county by the landowners. A few, however, did not want the road. In these cases, the county tried to work out deals with the owners before using its power of imminent domain. When a Mr. Brown did not want the road on his land, the county agreed to buy this land for $30.50.

Many challenges occurred along the way to getting the road completed. When they made it to the George Wythe School, the workmen turned the road south, which would cut off a portion of the playground. It turned out the workmen had been given the wrong plans. That section of road was filled in and routed to the north side of the school's playground. The curve they made was called "Dead Man's Curve," as the road had two ninety-degree turns around the Wythe School. Over the years, the county reworked that section of road many times to what we have today: a wide curve around the fire station and the Wythe Pool, which is the former site of the school.

Another issue that had to be resolved was that at the end near the Jackson Street Bridge (today's Sunset Creek bridge), the new road ended 1,600 feet short. The county did not want to pay for the new road to connect with the bridge, as it was within the city lines of Hampton. Hampton's Business Association supported the effort to pay for roadway that was needed to tie the two cities together. The association felt that if it worked to raise the funds, it would reap the benefits of having this new road connect with businesses in Hampton. The association called on the city council to ask for the $1,500 needed to continue the road. The city gave $500 to the cause, and the association was able to secure the remaining funds. The road was continued to the Jackson Street Bridge.

The road was completed in December 1909, only a few weeks after starting construction. The county waited until the following spring to hold a dedication celebration. At this event, the county renamed the road Kecoughtan Road after citizens had lobbied the county supervisors to name the road after the Kecoughtan village located in Hampton. The county records read, "Be it resolved by the Board of Supervisors of Elizabeth City County that the new road from Hampton to Newport News, being the first modern, permanently improved road in Elizabeth City County, is named the Kecoughtan Road in order to commemorate the name of the Indian village formerly standing in the present site of the City of Hampton."

It did not take long for the road to become the main artery of travel between both cities. By October 1910, citizens' groups were already asking the county to re-oil the road, as the heavy traffic had begun to take a toll on the roadbed by breaking the small stones away from its oil embedment. The county agreed to spend $150 from the liquor tax fund to make the necessary improvements.

In the fall of 1911, a local resident requested that the county install a streetlight in the center of the road near the George Wythe School. The light was approved, and in November of that year, it was installed. This light was turned on and off manually by Mr. Perkins, owner of the Perkins Store located on Claremont Avenue behind the Wythe School. Speed was always a concern for the roadway as automobile traffic increased. The first speed limit was set at twenty-two miles per hour. Citizens' groups soon became concerned with the speed, however, and asked the county supervisors for speed bumps, which were not approved.

General stores and gas stations were the first businesses to open along the fourteen-mile route. Automobile traffic continued to increase, and this took a toll on the road. Without the county aiding in its continued maintenance, the road by 1916 was in such disrepair that local business owners went to the city councils of Newport News and Hampton and the supervisors of Elizabeth City County to request that they apply for federal funding to repair the road. By October of that year, the road had deteriorated so badly that the Commonwealth highway engineer, after performing a survey, said that it was in need of immediate repairs and that it would have to be nearly completely resurfaced. During this time, the Wythe Protective Service

Early gas stations similar to this one, located near the intersection of Kecoughtan Road and Powhatan Parkway, dotted the Peninsula's Main Street. *Courtesy of Caroline Whiteed.*

asked the county to lease the road to the group and proposed to erect tolls in order to maintain the roadway. Its plan was to toll everyone who used the road except the residents of the Wythe District. This proposal was not well received by county supervisors and was quickly rejected. Kecoughtan Road was slowly repaired but was never rebuilt as the Commonwealth engineer had requested.

In the mid-1930s, developers Drucker and Falk came to Wythe and saw an opportunity to build on Kecoughtan Road. They decided to build two developments—the Kecoughtan Apartments and, across the street, a shopping plaza named the Wythe Shopping Center. At the last minute, the owners of the Palace Theater in Newport News decided to build a six-hundred-seat movie theater at the end of the shopping center. The shopping center would hold nine storefronts of varying sizes. Also included was a plan to build a small gas station in the southwest corner of the parking lot. Wythe Center opened in 1939 with Big Star Groceries at one end and the Wythe Theater at the other. The stores in between included Fields' Children and Gift Shop, La-Dor Beauty Shop, Hickory Salt Hamburger Restaurant, Ham's Brothers Bakery and Wythe Pharmacy. An Esso gas station was built in the corner of the parking lot. A few years later, a small hardware store

A group of Wythe residents having a five-cent Coca-Cola at the Wythe Pharmacy in the mid-1940s. *Courtesy of Kelly Siegel.*

The first of many food stores to occupy this location in Wythe Plaza. This picture was probably taken on a Sunday, judging by the lack of cars in the parking lot. *Courtesy of John Hugles.*

opened, and the Wythe Center was full. The shopping plaza was the first in what people called the suburbs of Hampton and Newport News.

The opening of the Wythe Center in 1939 spurred others to invest along Kecoughtan Road. With more stores, restaurants and other businesses opening up, Kecoughtan Road truly became the main street of the Lower Peninsula. The forty-plus businesses were located within several blocks and around the Wythe Center; this area comprised the Wythe Business District, which was situated between Pochin Place and Wythe Parkway. Storeowners and managers formed a group in order to pool their money and resources together for events and group advertising in the local papers, as well as to band to together to bring concerns to the county board of supervisors. This area was not the only place on Kecoughtan Road home to stores. Shops, restaurants and services of all kind opened in small clusters between homes from LaSalle Avenue to the Newport News city line.

In 1945, over 30 different businesses lined Kecoughtan Road from LaSalle Avenue to Pear Avenue. Twelve years later, over 120 businesses and services were listed in the same area. Following are the businesses you could have patronized if you lived in Olde Wythe in 1957, starting at Pear Avenue and running east to LaSalle Avenue. (To help identify where the businesses were located, we listed the block in which you would find them).

BUSINESSES ALONG THE PENINSULA'S "MAIN STREET": KECOUGHTAN ROAD

Pear Avenue
Boulevard Service Station
Blount's Refrigeration Repair; Economy Auto Sales
Wade Business Machines
Bill Bowditch Used Cars
Bilt-Rite Furniture and Upholstery

Cherry Avenue
Bowditch Motors
Kecoughtan Pharmacy
Gammon's Antique Shop
Bailey's Used Cars
Star Electric
Hamilton Arms Sporting Goods
Hills Seafood Market
Moore Grocery Store

Locust Avenue
Locust Avenue Amoco Service Station
Peninsula Dura-Clean Company
Hall Real Estate
Wythe Cleaners
Russell Liverman Real Estate

Greenbriar Avenue
Kecoughtan Market Grocers
L.G. Smith and Sons Service Station

Hollywood Avenue
Richardson's Market
Taubman's Auto Accessories
Cottonwood Amoco Gas
Kitt Music
Life Insurance Company of Virginia
Wythe Esso Service Station

Catalpa Avenue
Kelly Paint Company
Peninsula Electric Motor Service
Wythe Fire Station
High's Ice Cream Corporation

Pennsylvania Avenue
Bill's Barbecue
Wythe Amoco Service Station
Wythe Surplus Sales Store
Frost Hut Ice Cream
Kirby Vacuum Cleaners Sales and Service
Peninsula Electric Company
Superior Motors Incorporated
Rendezvous Restaurant
Riley's Barber Shop
Peninsula Hardware Company of Hampton
Peninsula Electric Company Contractors

Peninsula Electric Service, one of the many small businesses that made its home on the "Main Street" during the second half of the twentieth century. *Courtesy of Wayne and Mark Carr.*

Jackson Street
Wythe Mobil Gas Station
Dream House Furniture Company
Exotic Aquarium
Rowe Sheet Metal Works
Gene Edmonds Photography
Rosenbaum Memorial Park Cemetery
Phoebus Motor Company, Incorporated Autos
Wisco Storm Doors
Central Motor Company Used Cars
Wythe Florist
VIM Television and Appliance Sales and Service
Peninsula Maid Cabinet Makers
Grogan Service Station
Gordon Furniture Co.
B and W Used Cars
Garrett's Esso Service Center

Wythe Parkway
Wythe Recreation Center
Colonial Stores, Grocery Store
Dowden Insurance Agency
Wythe Auto Supply Company
Wythe Hardware Company
Wythe Sinclair Service Station
Wythe Sporting Goods
Wythe Lamp Repair and Supply Company
Field's Children's and Ladies Wear
Murray's Home Supplies
Wythe Appliance and Television
The Smart Shop
Wythe Restaurant
The Terry Gift Shop
Nodzak's Pastry Shop
CST Automatic Laundries
Wythe Men's Shop
Wellworth Cleaners
Wythe Pharmacy
Wythe Newsstand
Main's Little House Women and Children's Clothes
Wythe Taxi Stand
Wythe Theater

Chesterfield Road
Woolworth's
A&P Grocery
Virginia's Beauty Shop
Wythe Shoe Repair
Wythe Post Office
State Farm Insurance
Bank of Hampton Roads
Pocahontas Place
Pocahontas Service Station
Brown Derby Restaurant
Wythe Trailer Camp
Wythe Cleaners

Powhatan Parkway
Indian River Service Center
Wythe Medical Center
Kecoughtan Laundry and Cleaners
Warner Printing Company
G. Rosso's and Sons Wholesale Produce
Indian River Groceries

Pochin Place
Phelps Millinery Salon
The Nest Restaurant
Peninsula Caterers
Thomas Phillips Building Contractors
Wythe Tourist Home

Cherokee Road
High's Ice Cream Shop
W.C. Tice Locksmith Service
Kecoughtan Gift Shop
Poole's Barber Shop
Oasis Restaurant and Coffee Shop
The Chinese Restaurant
Hampton Colonial Place Radio and Television Service
Art's Confectionary
Gerald Freeman, Dentist
Franklin Freda, Physician
Time Craft Watch Repair

Brightwood Avenue
White Oak Lodge Restaurant
Crystal Garden Inn Restaurant

East Avenue
Gene Russell, Florist
Henkel Florist
Joe Weistead Real Estate

LaSalle Avenue
LaMar Steak House
Merrimac Motors

A few businesses/service providers that seemed to have touched the hearts of locals in the Wythe area were Bill's Barbecue, the Wythe Theater and the Wythe District Fire Department.

The Wythe Theater

The Wythe Theater opened on October 6, 1939, and was the first neighborhood theater house on the Peninsula. The construction, which cost $35,000, began in June of that year, with an anticipated opening date in July. However, due to a shortage of steel, the construction was slowed and the grand opening delayed. At first, the theater owners, the Gordons, who owned the Palace Theater in Newport News and went on to own others around the Peninsula, wanted the building to hold five hundred seats. Soon after the construction began, and after talking with residents of the area, the Gordons changed their minds and decided to make the building big enough to hold close to six hundred seats.

The new theater was built with all the modern amenities of the time. A local newspaper noted of the theater:

The seats have backs of upholstered mohair and bottoms of leather...and are 34 inches wide...the seats in one row are not directly behind those in the row in front and a clear vision of the screen is possible. Both the foyer and the auditorium are heavily carpeted. Both of the curtains, the eggshell screen curtain and the ornamental stage curtain, are operated by remote control from the projection booth. Indirect cone lighting is used in the auditorium. The lights are concealed in four troughs and the light bulbs are long and slender tubes. The amount of light is easily controlled and the direct lighting permits the desired amount of soft light in the auditorium at all times while no light fixtures are visible. To complete the comfort features is the lavishly furnished lounge, smoking room for men and a powder room for the women. The decoration of the entire theater was handled by the Novelty Scene studios of New York City and was carried out in the modernistic manner. The most modern Western Electric sound equipment is employed, and to improve the acoustics of the building, the ceiling was treated with a special acoustical plaster.

The Gordons advertised "ultra comfortable seats, air conditioning by Carrier, for year round comfort in a healthful atmosphere, and no parking worries—loads of car-room directly in front of the theater." They added a few new amenities that other theaters in Newport News or Hampton did not have. These included the installation of hearing devices on a dozen or so seats for patrons who were hard of hearing. In addition, the Gordons incorporated a spacious lounge area in the theater where local clubs and other organizations frequently met. The owners made a point to work with the civic groups of the area with promotions and reduced priced tickets. From the beginning, they made every effort to reach out to the community, of which they soon became an integral part.

The first movie shown at the theater was *The Rains Came*, starring Myrna Loy and Tyrone Powers. The local papers reported that a full house of 581 people were in attendance for the grand opening. The theater went on to show first-run movies until 1965.

The Wythe Theater was also a place where boys and girls in the neighborhood went to apply for jobs. Many became ushers, as during this time, all the movie houses had ushers, who walked the aisles with flashlights and made sure that patrons were behaving themselves. Other jobs for teens were ticket takers and concession stand attendants. It was a big deal if you were hired at the theater, as jobs for area youngsters were very competitive. The benefit that these young people enjoyed the most was free admission to all the movies when they were not on duty.

When the theater first opened, movies cost $0.25 for matinees. The evening show, which started at 6:00 p.m., cost $0.35. The children's price was only $0.10 for both matinee and evening shows. Later, in 1944, the admission cost for matinees was raised to $0.76 for adults, $0.55 for servicemen and $0.40 for children. The prices for evening shows were raised to $1.10 for adults, $0.75 for servicemen and $0.55 for children.

Saturday matinees were very popular with the Wythe children. Their parents would send them up to the movies in the afternoon, and they would spend the day watching movie shorts such as the Three Stooges, cartoons and a feature film, usually a western or science fiction movie.

In the early 1960s, the neighborhood started to change, and fewer residents were going to the movies at the Wythe Theater. In an effort to keep up with the changing times, the Wythe also started to change. The first change was made when the theater started to show second-run movies. The movie's first run was at the Palace Theater in Newport News for the first week of its release date, and it was then sent to the Wythe the second week.

A 1946 holiday advertisement showing the Wythe Theater staff. *Courtesy of Bill Saser.*

More change came when, on May 4, 1965, the Wythe Theater closed and was reopened a few days later as the Wythe Cinema, the new term being used in place of the word "theater" across the county.

By the late 1960s and into the 1970s, the number of movie theaters in Hampton grew. The Wythe Cinema continued to show movies, but attendance dwindled. At one time in the '70s, it started showing X-rated movies, but this was not a regular occurrence.

With over a dozen choices of movie theaters in Hampton and Newport News, competition for business was fierce, and the Wythe owners tried numerous strategies to drum up business. On January 16, 1980, the local paper reported that the Wythe would close for remodeling. The theater was reopened on January 18 as a one-dollar movie house, showing the movie *Alien*. Monday through Friday, the theater had only one showing, at 7:00 p.m. On Saturdays and Sundays, it would have three showings starting at 3:00 p.m. The last one-dollar movie shown was on August 3, 1980, when the theater showed *Invasion of the Body Snatchers*. On August 4, 1980, the Wythe became a two-dollar theater with the showing of the movie *The Slammers*. The owners decided to close the Wythe Theater in mid-March 1981; the final movie shown was *Black Vengeance*.

After the theater closed, the space was remodeled into a storefront. Over the years, it has been rented to several different retail stores. The space has been the home of Advance Auto Parts since 2003.

BILL'S BARBECUE

If you asked ten people over the age of forty about their favorite place to eat while growing up in Wythe or on the Peninsula, nine out of the ten would say Bill's Barbecue. Everyone who ate there loved the homemade barbecue, milk shakes and other menu items.

For over sixty years, from 1932 until 1999, Bill's Barbecue was located next to the Wythe fire station at the curve along Kecoughtan Road that was once called Dead Man's Curve (the curve has been rerouted over the decades to make it safer).

The restaurant opened in August 1932 and was named "Bill's" after a cook who was hired by its first owners, Fred and Pearle Hellums. The barbecue that everyone loved was his recipe.

For the grand opening of Bill's in the summer of 1934, Fred hired a traveling stuntman whose specialty was being buried alive. Bob Cutchuns Jr., who grew up in Wythe during the 1930s, remembered the stunt like it was yesterday:

He was in a pine box with two square stacks, one at his head and the other at his feet. The shafts were about six inches by six inches and were used for ventilation, for lowering food and reading items and for removal of waste. The "coffin" had electric power, so he was able to have lights and a radio. Once he was in the box, the men started to shovel dirt in the hole. The next morning, after waking up, my brother and cousin and I ran over to Bill's to see if the man was still in the box. When we got there, we heard the radio playing. I think he was down there for about four days. Once I lowered down a Coke to him, he drank it, and I pulled the empty bottle back up. Each day the crowds became bigger and bigger. After the fourth day, they dug him up, and when he got out, he was so stiff he could hardly walk. One of the first things he said was, "I need a shot of whiskey."

In the 1930s, Bill's became the place to go for good barbecue and pork steaks along with a delicious malt. The barbecue rotisseries were located outside in the back corner of the restaurant and would fill the air with a smoky scent. With the Wythe School so close by, many of the students would enjoy the scent in the air. For the older students, a quick dash to Bill's after school was a top priority.

The Hellumses owned Bill's until 1951, when the White family bought the business. The Whites were not your average couple looking for a business to buy. These folks knew the restaurant business. Just down the street from Bill's, Mr. White had opened a burger and hotdog stand called the White Derby. While Mr. White ran the White Derby in Wythe, Mrs. White was running another White Derby near the Newport News Shipyard, serving workers and anyone else who enjoyed a good hamburger or hotdog.

After purchasing Bill's, both of the White Derby restaurants were closed, and Mr. and Mrs. White worked together at the new restaurant. They lived in the upstairs apartment for a short while until they started their family. They first built a home along the James River.

The restaurant was open from 7:00 a.m. to 11:00 p.m. It was a hit with the young crowd, who would come after school for a snack or stop in after dates or football games. The breakfasts and lunches were very popular, and the restaurant quickly became the place to be if you wanted to hear what was going on in the community. When men came home from the war, Bill's was one of the first stops they would make, as it was a taste of home that they had missed while serving overseas.

Each cook at the restaurant had his own special recipe on the menu board. One cook had a secret recipe for chicken salad and would not share it with the other cooks, so that cook was the only one who made that salad. Others would add their touches to menu items, and the Whites just let them have fun as long as those items sold. If the dish did not sell well, it was not offered again.

Bill's had a few firsts for the area. It had the first curbside service, where waitresses would take your order at your car and bring it out to you so you would not have to go in. Some of the girls would use roller skates to get around, but most just walked. The signs on Bill's were not to be mistaken. A giant whale welcomed the guests with the saying, "Whale of a Meal." Other signs advertised the barbecue, while still others offered a larger version of the menu that could be read by folks in their cars. One of the most favorite and most remembered signs were the little pink pigs that spelled out "barbecue" running across the front of the restaurant. Bill's was one of the first businesses in the area to use neon lights, which were much brighter than just having spotlights shining on the signs like everyone else along Kecoughtan Road.

During the 1950s and '60s, the Whites became friendly with the Maloney family, owners of the Williamsburg Pottery. Each spring, the

This was the first *Daily Press* advertisement for Bill's Barbecue taken out by new owners Jimmy and Jo White. *Courtesy of Myra Vick.*

Whites would bring in trucks from the pottery filled with planters and garden statuary, which they would then sell to their customers. If you drove past Bill's during this time of year, you would see these items lined up around the building.

The Whites were very good to their staff. All of the employees worked part time, and the Whites would help them out if they needed medical

It is reported that this was the first business on the Peninsula to have outside neon lighting. *Courtesy of Myra Vick.*

attention or clothes. These acts of kindness made working at Bill's enjoyable and made the staff members feel like they were part of the family, which, in turn, made them loyal to the Whites. Staff members often worked at Bill's for years, a few staying over thirty years.

The Whites had one daughter, Myrna, who, along with her mother, took a leading role in running the family restaurant when her father died in the 1972. When Myrna's mother died, she ran Bill's for a while and then decided it was time to sell and move on with her life with her husband and growing family.

In 1975, the restaurant was sold to Mr. Dowden and Mr. Edwards, who went on to remodel it for the first time since it opened in 1934. The keys to Bill's were handed over to Nita Mitchell, the daughter of Mr. Dowden. For over twenty-four years, Mitchell ran Bill's with the same great food and service as the Whites and the Hellumses before her. She did add her own touches to the restaurant, including adding submarine sandwiches to the menu and changing the name to Bill's Barbecue and Subs. Another one of the additions Mitchell brought to Bill's was carving out a semiprivate room in the restaurant called the "Pig Pen" where small groups would meet. In this room, shelves of a growing collection of pigs were on display, many being added by customers. Signs that had a pig motif also dotted the room.

One that Mike Cobb of the Hampton History Museum remembers said, "Never try to teach a pig to sing…because it wastes your time and irritates the pig!"

In an interview with the local paper on the closing of Bill's, Mitchell said that a lot of Hampton women worked there in the summer as teens and came back to work as adults. One cook named Estelle Howard had worked at Bill's for forty-five years before it closed. She joked that she came with the building. Right up to the very end, the barbecue recipe remained the same, as did other familiar items on the menu, a testament to a place that became one of the most beloved restaurants on the Peninsula's main street, Kecoughtan Road.

THE WYTHE DISTRICT FIRE DEPARTMENT

The Wythe District Fire Department had its beginnings in 1909, when the Wythe Protection Association, a local civic group, gave permission for a fire station to be built next to its association building fronting Kecoughtan Road. Funds were secured, and a one-story fire station was erected.

The Wythe department was not the only one in the area. The other one was the Riverview Volunteer Fire Department, which was organized on February 12, 1910, with forty members. Riverview was the most populated part of the Wythe District at this time. This area, which stretched from Shell Road to Bay Avenue, had forty-nine dwellings, three stores, a small school and two churches. Two of the trustees, Mr. and Mrs. Fraley, deeded a lot on Darnaby Avenue to the department "for as long as the organization was active in the extinguishing of fires in the community." On the endorsement of personal notes from the members, money was secured to build a twenty-foot- by twenty-foot, one-story frame building. To get started, the company received a reel and hose from the Hampton Fire Department, as well as two rubber buckets, helmets, boots and coats.

In 1913, Riverview built a hose wagon that could be pulled by either horses or men. This wagon carried 750 feet of hose. In 1915, Riverview purchased two fifty-gallon chemical tanks and mounted them on a Ford chassis. This was one of the first motorized fire apparatuses in Virginia.

As both the Riverview and Wythe Fire Departments grew, they received financial support from banks, businesses, private citizens and the county.

However, a large portion of the company's income came from activities sponsored by an entertainment committee that held oyster suppers, ice cream socials, smokers, dances, trolley rides and turkey shoots. In 1921, with a decline in membership in both companies due to World War I and the financial burden to keep the departments running, the Riverview Volunteer Fire Department drew up a bill to present to the citizens of the Wythe District that would levy a tax for firefighting and maintaining a water supply. After receiving the support of the citizens, the county's representative in the House of Delegates was notified of the action and requested a special election. The election was held in August 1922, and the voters decided to levy a tax of $0.10 per $100 property value for firefighting purposes.

Early in 1923, the two companies merged under the name "Wythe District Fire Department." Meetings were held in the Wythe Protection Association building to work out the details of the merged companies. Bills were paid and surplus apparatus disposed of, and the lot on Darnaby Street that the Riverview department was using was returned to Mr. and Mrs. Farley. The engine house of the Wythe company became the new headquarters, and the trucks from the Riverview company became the principal fire trucks for the new department. The department soon outgrew the quarters adjacent to the Wythe Protective Association, and in February 1932, the county provided larger quarters at the old Hooper-Hardy garage across the street. The new department moved in the following month. In 1939, efforts were made to secure better quarters for the department; however, progress was not made until October 1944, when ground was broken for a new station. The new station on Kecoughtan Road was opened in May 1945 and is still being used today.

But the Wythe District Fire Department was solely that—a fire department. It wasn't until 1939 that the Wythe Fire Company Rescue Squad was started. A first-aid class taught in 1937 was the spark that made the Wythe District Fire Department first-aid conscious, and it resulted in the formation of a first-aid committee. This committee was charged with continuing the training and maintaining the first-aid kits carried on the fire apparatuses to give first aid to its members and to citizens injured at fires. The station had a 1924 Packard car that had been converted to a fire truck some years back, and it reused this vehicle and had it equipped with first-aid supplies. Soon a call came in to the station that people were injured in an auto accident near the Kecoughtan Apartments on Kecoughtan Road. This was the first call that the new first-aid truck received. Lacerations of the injured were bandaged, and a broken leg splinted. An injured man was transported to Dixie Hospital, and the Wythe

District Fire Department Rescue Squad was born. The Packard was used until August 1940, when the Dixie Hospital donated a Buick ambulance to the squad. Although the ambulance was as old as the Packard, it permitted its driver, crew and patients to be sheltered from the elements. The ambulance was painted bright red and served until 1943.

Soon the volunteer fire department and rescue squad members became paid professionals of the city of Hampton. Volunteers are still part of the Wythe station today, but they are used to supplement the paid members as they learn fire and first-aid techniques for a possible career with the city fire department. In 2005, the Hampton City Fire Department began a search for a new site to replace the now outdated 1945 Wythe station. The first choice for a new location, the lot that had once been home to Wythe Cleaners at the corner of Kecoughtan Road and Powhatan Parkway, was deemed unusable. As of the publication of this book, the city is still working on finding a suitable building lot to locate a new station somewhere in the Wythe District.

The "Main Street" we see today is a far cry from what it was in its heyday. Many things are to blame for the change. The Kecoughtan Corridor Master Plan developed by the City of Hampton is a way to address revitalizing the once busy business district. The goal of the city is to transform the road into a residential street with a few small shopping "pods" in between. The beginning of this transformation is what we see today. The open lots once held thriving businesses that closed. The city purchased the buildings from the owners, tore them down and planted grass in the open lots. Once the city acquires enough lots that can be combined, it will begin searching for developers to build homes in the style of the neighborhood along the former "Main Street of the Peninsula."

Chapter 8

KIT HOMES IN OLDE WYTHE

In the early 1900s, you could order just about anything from a mail-order catalogue: plows, obesity powders, the Heidelberg electric belt (the 1900s cure for male problems), sewing machines, cookstoves and even complete houses. In 1895, Sears issued its first building materials catalogue and began selling lumber, hardware, millwork and other building materials in addition to the tens of thousands of items already offered in its general merchandise mail-order catalogue. In 1908, a headline on page 594 of the catalogue read, "$100 Set of Building Plans Free. Let Us Be Your Architect without Cost to You." Customers were invited to write in and ask for a copy of Sears' new *Book of Modern Homes and Building Plans*, which featured house plans and building materials.

Today, Sears (with headquarters in northern Illinois) is the most well known of the kit house companies, but it was neither the first nor the largest—those honors go to Aladdin. After all these years, the name "Aladdin Homes" (Bay City, Michigan) might not be a familiar one, and yet Aladdin issued its first mail-order house catalogue in 1906, two years before Sears. And while Sears was out of the kit house business by 1940, Aladdin continued to sell mail-order kit homes until 1981. During its thirty-two years in the kit home business, Sears sold fewer than seventy thousand homes. By contrast, more than seventy-five thousand Aladdin Homes were built. "Sears kit homes" has almost become a generic, catchall phrase, which is unfortunate (and not accurate). In the early 1900s, there were seven companies selling kit homes on a national level. In addition to Sears and Aladdin, there were

Gordon Van Tine (based in Davenport, Iowa), Montgomery Ward (Chicago, Illinois), Harris Brothers (Chicago, Illinois), Sterling Homes (Bay City, Michigan) and Lewis Manufacturing (also in Bay City).

The Brentwood was a classic Arts and Crafts, two-story kit home first offered by Aladdin in the 1910s. It was one of the company's finest homes, with about 1,800 square feet, a grand entry hall, four bedrooms and a second-floor balcony off the master bedroom. Unlike the Brentwoods in other parts of the country, the house pictured in Olde Wythe appears much like it did when it first graced the cover of the 1913 Aladdin Homes catalogue.

Less than a block away is another spacious and grand kit home, the Aladdin Shadow Lawn. Like the Brentwood, the Shadow Lawn is in stunningly original condition, with cypress clapboards on the first story and cedar shakes on the upper floor. Fortunately, the aluminum siding salesmen had not yet had their way with this beauty, and the home's dramatic proportions (including those distinctive three-foot-deep eaves) were still very much in evidence. Further down Powhatan Parkway is a Wardway Lexington, an imposing two-story Dutch Colonial and one of the finest kit homes that Montgomery Ward offered during its thirty-one years in the kit house business.

Olde Wythe contains more than two dozen kit homes from Aladdin, Montgomery Ward, Gordon Van Tine and Sears, as well as a couple from Lewis Manufacturing and Harris Brothers. How did this early twentieth-century neighborhood in Hampton, Virginia, end up with more than two dozen mail-order kit homes from six different companies? It is an intriguing question. This high concentration of kit homes in a small area is more reminiscent of what is found in a midwestern suburb (where many of these mail-order companies were located), but Hampton, Virginia? In southeastern Virginia, there are more kit homes from Aladdin than from any other company. While Aladdin had its corporate headquarters in Bay City, it also had a massive mill in Wilmington, North Carolina, about four hours south of Hampton.

Based on stories from other parts of the country, it seems that kit homes really did sell themselves. It took just one homeowner building one house to get folks' attention far and wide. After all, it'd be hard not to be curious when your neighbor takes delivery of a twelve-thousand-piece kit and starts sorting out the pieces and parts on an empty lot. When the wooden kegs with 750 pounds of nails came out, and something resembling a house started to take shape, it was only a matter of time before pedestrians and streetcar commuters started paying attention. Judging by the ebullient testimonials that fill the back pages of the old catalogues, it seems that there really was an

The Brentwood. *Courtesy of Rosemary Thornton.*

The Shadow Lawn. *Courtesy of Rosemary Thornton.*

abundance of genuinely satisfied customers who couldn't wait to spread the good news of their beautiful new mail-order kit homes, built with their own hands and made with the very finest of building materials.

It only took one bold soul to take the plunge and order a house—sight unseen—from a mail-order catalogue, and after that, the locals would have an opportunity to inspect the quality of the building materials firsthand and see that the lumber really was first rate. And then, perhaps they'd be willing to make a few inquiries of their own with Aladdin, Sears or one of the other companies. And there were significant financial benefits to building your own kit home. Typically, a pre-cut kit home could be built for about 35 percent less than a traditional stick-built house. For many, that was enough to bring the price of homeownership within their grasp. Sears' oft-stated promise that your new house payment could be "cheaper than rent" was not mere puffery; it was a solid fact.

These catalogues were expensive to publish but proved to be popular—and enduring. They're not free anymore, but for about $100, you can still pick them up at online auction sites and in antique bookstores. These 120-plus-page catalogues were the original wish book, and today, they offer a quaint look at life in America a century ago. "Own your own home and make your dreams come true," read the first pages of the 1928 Sears *Modern Homes* catalogue. "Get your share of contentment for yourself and for your kiddies that comes only after you live in a home of your own. Payments as low as $35 a month." Most of these vintage catalogues have ciphering in the margins, where Mama was figuring out if she could afford the Hercules Steam Heating Outfit or if she'd have to settle for the "Pipeless Furnace" (a coal-fired space heater)—or maybe Father was trying to figure out how to stretch the budget so they could get the most house for the money. It's a testimony to the success of mail-order marketing that now, more than one hundred years later, these catalogues have become collectors' items and are highly sought after. With all the complexities of today's modern world, it's hard to imagine that you could sit down with a catalogue and order a house through the mail, but Sears (always a leader in marketing everything from cream separators to corsets) made the process quite simple.

After receiving the catalogue and selecting a house design, buyers were asked to send in a "$1 good faith deposit." In return, they'd receive by mail a detailed building materials list and full blueprints. If they liked what they saw, they'd send in the balance of monies owed, minus the one-dollar deposit. If the novice homebuilder needed a mortgage, there was a one-page mortgage application in the back of the catalogue that was to be turned in with the order. Sears asked only two financial questions of potential buyers: "Do you have a vocation?" and "Do you own the lot on which you intend to build?" If the answer to both questions was "yes," you qualified for a 75 percent mortgage (the lot accounted for the remaining 25 percent).

A few weeks after the order was placed, a railroad boxcar—filled to the roofline with building materials—would arrive at the nearest train depot. If an "already-cut and fitted home" (first offered in 1915) was purchased, the framing members—joists, rafters and studs—were pre-cut and ready to be nailed into place. This represented a tremendous saving of time and money for the homebuilder. The electric circular saw that every homeowner cherishes was not widely marketed until the late 1920s. Each piece of pre-cut lumber was stamped with a letter and numbers to facilitate assembly. A seventy-five-page leather-bound instruction book, with the homeowner's name embossed in gold on the cover, gave precise directions on the proper placement of those twelve thousand pieces of house. The book offered this somber warning: "Do not take anyone's advice as to how this building should be assembled."

In 1908, Sears estimated that a carpenter would charge $450.00 to erect a two-story Foursquare house with a hipped roof and a lone shed dormer in the attic. However, Sears also promised that a man with an elementary understanding of construction techniques would be able to assemble the house. About half the people who purchased a Sears kit home hired a contractor to build it. The other half read their seventy-five-page instruction book very carefully. According to Sears' calculations, a painter would charge $34.50 to paint a typical 1,600-square-foot two-story house. The plasterer's bill would be around $200.00, which included nailing up 840 square yards of wooden lath and applying three coats of plaster. Masonry (block, brick, cement) and plaster were not included in the kit (due to shipping costs) and were to be obtained locally.

The term "modern home" was part of the vernacular in the early 1900s, as portrayed by Sears Alhambra design, which sold for $2,674. It was a descriptive term indicating that a house had modern amenities (that we take for granted today) such as a heating system, electricity and indoor plumbing. In some cases, the houses were more modern than the communities in which they were built. Electricity and municipal water systems were not available in every locale where Sears homes were sold. To meet this need, Sears offered bathroom-less houses well into the 1920s. And for about $30, you could always purchase a dandy outhouse. This also explains, in part, why Sears sold heating, electrical and plumbing equipment separately and not as part of the kit. These homes were sold in all forty-eight states, thus a homeowner in northern Wisconsin would need a very different heating system than one in Hampton, Virginia. Sears promised that a "man of average abilities" could have the house completed in ninety days. If you obtained a mortgage from Sears, you were required to have the house ready for occupancy in four months. Failure to do so meant that you'd forfeit the mortgage.

The very details that make early twentieth-century kit homes so unique can also help with the identification process these many decades later:

1) Look for stamped lumber in the basement or attic. As mentioned above, the framing members were stamped with a letter and a number to help facilitate construction. The lumber in Aladdin homes was marked with a word (such as "rafter," "joist" or "roof"). Today, those marks can help establish that your house started life as a mail-order kit.

2) Look for shipping labels. These are often found on the back of millwork (baseboard molding, door and window trim, etc). In the case of Sears, the label might read "Sears & Roebuck," but more typically it reads, "Return address, 925 Homan Avenue, Chicago, Illinois."

3) Look in the attic and basement for any paperwork (original blueprints, letters, etc.) that might reveal that you have a kit home. These can sometimes be found tucked away in attics or behind built-in cabinetry.

4) Courthouse records. From 1911 to 1933, Sears offered mortgages on its kit houses. Using grantee records, you might find a few Sears mortgages and thus a few Sears homes.

5) Plumbing and hardware fixtures. Post-1930 Sears homes often have a small circled "SR" cast into the bathtub in the lower corner (farthest from the tub spout and near the floor) and on the underside of the kitchen or bathroom sink. In Aladdin homes, you might the word "Aladdin" on the doorknobs.

6) Goodwall sheet plaster. This was an early quasi-sheetrock product offered by Sears in the 1910s and '20s. The word "Goodwall" appears on the back of the sheet plaster, and this can be a clue that you might have a kit home.

Why were so many kit homes built in Olde Wythe? In the first years of the twentieth century, when these houses were being bought and built, the citizens

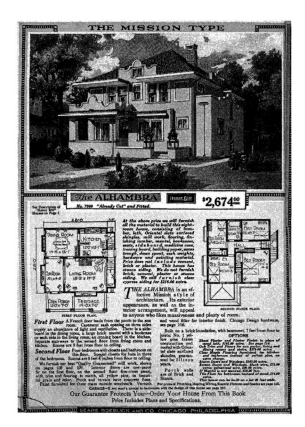

The Alhambra. *Courtesy of Rosemary Thornton.*

of Olde Wythe were employed at the local shipyards, seafood industries and government. Between work, church, social gatherings and school functions, there would have been many opportunities to discuss this radical and newfangled idea of ordering a kit house from a mail-order catalogue. In other communities where large collections of kit homes have been discovered, it's typically because of "word of mouth" and good testimonials. A happy, enthusiastic customer is always the best salesman, and the people who sacrificed and toiled and labored to buy and build a home with their own two hands really did fall in love with them. As one representative testimonial stated in the back pages of the Sears catalogue, "My Sears home is an ornament to the street on which it is located." Another happy homeowner wrote, "Everyone says I have the best and nicest house in town. Men from the local lumber mill say they cannot get such good lumber anywhere."

Sears, Aladdin, Gordon Van Tine and the others earned a well-deserved reputation for providing superior-quality lumber for both framing and millwork, and they were proud of their reputation. Exterior sidings were offered in red cedar, redwood or cypress. Interior floors were typically oak on the first floor, maple in the kitchens and baths and yellow pine on the second floor. The lumber for these houses came from America's first-growth, virgin forests, where trees grew naturally and slowly, competing for water

Example of numbered lumber. *Courtesy of Rosemary Thornton.*

and nutrients. The quality of building materials found in an early twentieth-century kit home is the likes of which we will never again see in this country.

When potential homebuyers saw that the lumber and building materials really were first rate, the only remaining questions were: Do I have the skills to build my own house? Are the directions clear? Can I find someone to help me get it done within four months? I imagine such questions were the topic of much conversation at the shipyards, docks and business offices throughout Hampton. And what better way to pass the day than to talk about the fact that you recently achieved a long-cherished dream of becoming a homeowner?

Of the twenty-one kit homes found in Olde Wythe, which one was the first? It's hard to know, but it's likely that one of the earliest houses was that beautiful Aladdin Brentwood on Powhatan Parkway. This model was first offered in the 1913 Aladdin Homes catalogue and last appeared in the 1919 catalogue. According to the Hampton City Directory, one of the home's early owners was an electrician, Harvey Franklin Sr. In the early 1900s, an electrician would have been a busy fellow and a popular man, as people were just starting to fully understand the marvels of an electrified domicile. It's plausible that Mr. Franklin was well known throughout the Olde Wythe community. Was it Mr. Franklin who spread the happy word about the quality of mail-order kit homes and the ease with which those twelve thousand pieces and parts could be assembled? It wouldn't have taken long for word to get out that it was the Franklin family who was building that beautiful two-story Arts and Crafts home on Pocahontas Street. One hundred years later, it's impossible to know for sure, but it seems likely that it was Mr. Franklin—or a progressive-minded resident like him—who showed his neighbors that buying and building your own kit home was the way to go. One hundred years from now, with some regular maintenance and a little love and thoughtful attention, it's likely that Mr. Franklin's Brentwood will still be standing proud and true. These houses were built with love and were intended to last for generations. Let's hope the story of their unique and humble beginnings will endure as well.

The following homes in Olde Wythe have been identified as homes constructed from mail-order kits:

113 Hampton Roads Avenue (MW Priscilla)
128 Hampton Roads Avenue (MW Priscilla)
136 Hampton Roads Avenue (MW Priscilla)
227 Hampton Roads Avenue (MW Priscilla)
2911 Chesapeake Avenue (GVT/MW Priscilla)

58 Shenandoah Road (Lewis Montawk)
76 Cherokee Road (Sears Alhambra)
138 Pochin Place (Aladdin Sheffield)
105 Pocahontas Place (Sears Hathaway)
137 Powhatan Parkway (Wardway Lexington)
65 Locust Street (Sears Berwyn)
139 Powhatan Parkway (Aladdin Marsden)
117 Locust Street (Aladdin Marsden)
105 Powhatan Parkway (Aladdin Shadow Lawn)
138 Pochin Place (Aladdin Sheffield)
114 Pear Avenue (Wardway Claremont)
45 Orchard Avenue (Sears Avondale)
1015 Blair Avenue (Aladdin Capitol)
125 Powhatan Parkway (Aladdin Brentwood)
81 Algonquin Road (Aladdin Plaza)
118 Pocohontas Place (Lewis Shelbourne)

Chapter 9

THE LINKS OF WYTHE

It's hard to imagine that between 1896 and 1920, about 25 percent of the land in the Olde Wythe neighborhood was home to one of the leading golf courses in the South. From Hampton Roads Avenue to East Avenue, and bordered by Kecoughtan Road and Chesapeake Avenue, the Hampton Roads Golf and Country Club was the place to meet and befriend business and political leaders from the cities of Hampton and Newport News, military officers from Fort Monroe and the many guests of the hotels at Old Point Comfort.

Golf had its beginnings in the United States in 1889, when the first "modern" golf club opened in Yonkers, New York. The game's popularity slowly grew, with approximately one hundred clubs opening by 1895. On October 7, 1896, a group of men, meeting at the Hotel Chamberlin at Old Point Comfort, formed the Hampton Roads Golf and Country Club. The group announced that the course would be located off Electric Avenue (now known as Victoria Boulevard) on land belonging to William Armstrong, the brother of General Samuel Chapman Armstrong, who had founded the Hampton Normal and Agricultural School. The links, to be laid out overlooking Hampton Roads, would be just a few blocks' walk from the intersection of Electric Avenue and Ammonate Park Avenue (which was later changed to Hampton Roads Avenue), near the main trolley line between Hampton and Newport News. Plans included building a clubhouse on the land as well. The group also announced that a professional golfer from Scotland had been hired and was busy mapping out the course. A grand opening was planned for the end of October.

The first officers of the club included:

President: Lieutenant James A. Shipton of Ironton, Ohio
Vice-President: Matthew Armstrong of Hampton, Virginia
Secretary/Treasurer: Lieutenant William B. Homer of Brookline, Massachusetts
Directors: Richard Armstrong of Hampton, Virginia; George W. Swett of Old Point Comfort, Virginia; and Lieutenant J.S. Lyon of Petersburg, Virginia

The nine-hole course, starting and ending near the clubhouse, covered approximately ten acres. Using the terrain of the area with its dips and valleys, small creeks and marshland among the flat areas, bunkers were dug out to make the course more challenging. During heavy rains, most of the course was under water, with the creeks overflowing and the marshland deep in mud.

Each fairway had its own name and unique hazards. Heading east from the clubhouse, the first hole, called "Vanity Fair," was 234 yards long with one bunker. Continuing east, hole two, called "Great Expectations," was 319 yards long and had one bunker. Turning and heading toward Hampton Roads, the third hole, called "Fool's Errand," was the longest at 445 yards and included a large bunker and a ditch. Hole four, called "Easy Street," headed west along Hampton Roads and included a 220-yard fairway with a bunker. The holes were then laid out in a zigzag pattern back to the clubhouse. Hole five, called "Rip Rap," had one bunker and a dip, while hole six, called "Prairie," included a double bunker and flat terrain. Holes seven and eight were named "Chilcoat Pass" at 288 yards and "Hopson's Choice" at 256 yards, respectfully. Each of these holes had deep ditches and swamp/marshland to overcome. Once through the middle holes, the ninth and final hole, called "Santigo," ran straight for 304 yards and brought golfers back toward the clubhouse. Players had to cross a footbridge that was built over a small creek to get to the clubhouse. The green and tee boxes were square, and the flag sticks were made of steel, about three feet tall and painted red with a heart-shaped design on top and the hole number in white in the middle of the heart.

The clubhouse was built facing Hampton Roads, which allowed wide views of the golf links and of passing ships in the harbor. The building was one story high with eight Georgia pine–paneled rooms, the largest being the dining room. Other rooms included lounges with open fireplaces and the finest furnishings, meeting rooms, a kitchen area and changing rooms.

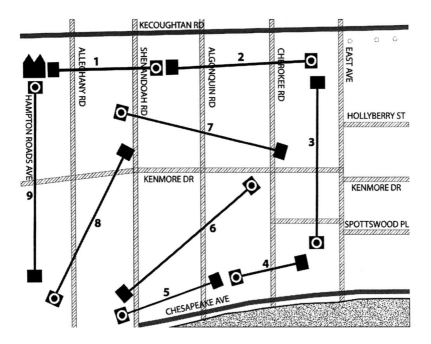

A diagram overlaying the links of the Hampton Roads Golf and Country Club on a map of today's Olde Wythe. *Courtesy of Greg Siegel.*

A view of the clubhouse, circa 1898. *Courtesy of Greg Siegel.*

ON THE
GOLF LINKS

An early postcard from 1900 sold by the Chamberlin Hotel and featuring the Hampton golf links. The two houses shown on the postcard insert can still be seen on Chesapeake Avenue. *Courtesy of Greg Siegel.*

The front porch was twenty feet deep and ran the fifty-foot length of the clubhouse. Tennis was another up-and-coming sport of the day, and this did not go without notice. Tennis courts were added to the east side of the clubhouse and were used for both recreation and tournaments.

In December 1896, the Hampton Roads Golf and Country Club was chartered in the Elizabeth City County Charter Book #1. The public grand opening was held on January 30, 1897. On February 6, 1897, players from as far away as Baltimore traveled to participate in the first tournament. Afterward, there was a reception in the clubhouse, with music provided by the Fort Monroe Artillery School Band. The Hampton Roads Golf and Country Club had quickly become the place to be with the "who's who" of both Hampton and Newport News, as well as with many of the army and navy officers from Fort Monroe.

In 1898, the management of the Hotel Hygeia and the Hotel Chamberlin at Old Point Comfort made an agreement with the club to offer use of the course as one of the amenities available to their guests, since other major hotel resorts along the East Coast also had golf available for their patrons. Through advertising in magazines and newspapers across the country, the hotels highlighted the fact that they offered golf throughout the year. Advertising in fall and winter emphasized the mild weather and touted the

Hampton Roads Golf and Country Club as *the* place to play golf in the South. As another way to promote golf as an amenity, the Chamberlin offered three different picture postcards of the course for purchase in its gift shop.

The club received its charter from the state of Virginia in 1899. That year, and again in 1900 and in 1912, the U.S. Golf Association featured the club in its monthly publication, including pictures of the clubhouse and photos taken to showcase the links. The articles described the course and clubhouse and detailed the area's rich American history. The major railroad companies in the East, as well as the Old Dominion Steamship Company, also featured the club in their brochures. These pamphlets highlighted what the traveler could see and do while visiting the area and also emphasized the mild winter weather to entice travelers to visit the area during this time of year.

In 1899, the famous British golf champion Harry Vardon dominated golf in Europe, winning nearly 75 percent of the matches and tournaments in which he participated. Vardon also had won his third British Open (he would go on to win a total of six, a record still held to this day). With his accuracy and control with the golf clubs, he was labeled "the greatest to ever play golf."

In America, the sport of golf received a huge boost in popularity when Vardon toured the country in 1900. Recognizing his appeal, Spalding Sporting Goods Company signed Vardon to promote a set of clubs modeled after those he used, as well as a new golf balls called the "Vardon Flyer." This also allowed Vardon to display his skills against all the top players in America. With this opportunity, Vardon became the world's first sports celebrity and golf's first international celebrity.

While on tour, Vardon played a total of eighty-eight matches, losing only fourteen of them. He also visited sporting goods stores, where he would drive golf balls into nets, show off his putting skills and sign autographs. He was able to bring the game of golf closer to thousands of people. American audiences admired Vardon's ability to powerfully hit golf balls high into the air and at long distances. He later wrote that "the Americans were not sufficiently advanced [in golf] to appreciate the finer points of the game. They did, however, appear to thoroughly enjoy the type of ball I drove. I hit it high for carry, which resembled a home run."

In early March 1900, Vardon was signed to play an exhibition match at the Hampton Roads Golf Club. The match was scheduled for March 30. A week before the match, he still did not have an opponent. Finally, Willie Dunn, the 1894 U.S. champion, agreed to play even though he was already scheduled to meet Vardon two weeks later. The match with Dunn was widely anticipated, as he was one player who Vardon had not beaten.

The club sent telegraphs to newspapers around the state to publicize the upcoming match. A special train was sent from Richmond to Old Point Comfort, and ferries brought over golfers and fans across Hampton Roads from Norfolk. The president of the Newport News Shipyard and the president of the Newport News, Hampton and Old Point Railroad sent their private streetcars to Old Point Comfort to bring distinguished guests staying at the Chamberlin Hotel to the golf club for the match.

Unfortunately, the weather did not cooperate, and a major storm moved in a couple days before the match, bringing heavy winds and rains. With the links laid out through valleys, creeks and marshes, more than a few holes were played with standing water and mud, adding additional obstacles to the bunkers around the links. A strong wind (twenty knots) was blowing the day of the match, and low temperatures made watching difficult for the approximately five hundred spectators.

The match began at 10:00 a.m. and finished by 1:00 p.m. Originally scheduled to play thirty-six holes, they ended up playing only twenty-seven. Vardon won 113 stokes to Dunn's 129. Vardon set two club records, one for longest drive on Fool's Errand (240 yards) and the other for the lowest score for nine holes (38 strokes). Following a catered lunch, a handicap tournament was held in which golfers who watched Vardon play tested their skills in an attempt to beat Vardon and Dunn's scores. The Old Dominion Steamship Company gave a silver cup as the prize for the winner.

A week later, the club hosted a two-day tournament sponsored by the Old Dominion Steamship Company. Players from Hampton, Newport News, Norfolk and Richmond participated. At this tournament, golfers were still taking notice of Vardon's now famous cutouts in the turf and the difficulty of the drives that he made on Hopson's Choice and Chilicoat Pass. After the Old Dominion trophy was awarded, a match called the "Lobster Tournament" was held. During his visit, Vardon had been asked to predict the lowest score for this nine-hole tournament. Richard Armstrong was the winner with a low score of 56, the exact score Vardon had written.

At the turn of the century, there were only a few organized golf clubs in Virginia: the Hampton Roads Golf and Country Club, Lakeside Golf Club and Hermitage Golf Club in Richmond, Roanoke Country Club, University of Virginia Golf Club, Alexandria Golf Club, Washington Golf Club and the Norfolk Country Club. The development of relationships between these established clubs lead to the formation, in 1904, of the Virginia State Golf Association, one of the first state golf associations in the United States. The first statewide tournament, held in Norfolk, was won by Lakeside, who defeated Hampton. Over the years, the Hampton Roads club supported growth of the sport in the state by hosting Virginia Cup matches as well as the State Amateur matches. In 1904, Hampton also became an allied member of the U.S. Golf Association. At this time, the club's news was being published in newspapers along the East Coast, including the *New York Times* and the *Washington Post*. In addition, the club's secretary regularly sent news notices to leading golf and sports magazines that included the dates of tournaments the club was hosting and scores from past tournaments. With this publicity, the club became one of the premier courses in the South.

Membership at the club grew when a new streetcar line was built in 1904. The trolley line ran along the Hampton Roads Harbor from Newport News to Hampton, right past the golf course, and continued on to Fort Monroe and Buckroe Beach, thereby opening an opportunity for easier access to the links. More hotels in Hampton and Newport News took advantage of this new access to advertise that their hotels were near the golf club. In 1912, the Chesapeake Ferry Company established a ferry service to Norfolk and built a wharf close to the course. In addition, the automobile was also gaining popularity around this time. These three modes of transportation—the streetcar, the ferry and the automobile—made access to the golf club easier than ever.

The influx of golfers resulted in increased membership revenue from both local players and visitors, who paid a guest fee to play. With these funds, along with funding from the agreement with the hotels at Old Point, the clubhouse and grounds were updated. More grass was planted over the entire course, and trees were planted along the fairways. The clubhouse, remodeled twice since opening, became one of the finest places in the area to meet and socialize. With its wide view of the harbor from the front porch, cool breezes off the water and the most modern amenities of the times, it was also used by local service and social clubs to hold various functions such as dinners, dances and meetings.

The Hampton Roads Golf and Country Club was so successful that in 1914, when the Chesapeake Ferry Company moved its ferry berth to Newport News, the board of directors announced plans to buy the ferry dock and the land attached to it. They wanted to build a bigger clubhouse that included rooms for overnight guests next to the docks. They also wanted to upgrade the piers so smaller boats from larger ships docked in the harbor could come ashore. In May 1914, a fundraiser, featuring an Italian play by students from the Hampton Normal School, was held. For reasons unknown, the clubhouse plan was never realized.

One of the club's best-known players was Jim McMenamin. Jim, a son of James McMenamin, one of the club's charter members and a main figure in the growth of the Hampton crabbing industry, learned to play golf barefoot by caddying at a young age. Jim became so skilled at the game that in 1912, he won the state amateur championship. He went on to win the championship again in 1913, playing on the Hampton course. After college, he worked in the family seafood business but quickly decided that that was not for him. For a period of time, Jim managed the Hampton Roads Golf and Country Club. In 1926, he became the golf professional for the Norfolk County Club, and in 1931, he designed the James River County Club in Newport News. "Gentle Jim," as he was called, was known as one of the state's best players.

The Hampton Golf and Country Club's most distinguished player was President Woodrow Wilson. President Wilson's only documented visit was on May 15, 1915. However, based on eyewitness accounts, he played the course on more than a few different occasions.

The May 15 visit came as President Wilson's party was on its way down the Chesapeake Bay en route to New York City to review the Atlantic Fleet. President Wilson was under pressure from Congress and others to determine the course the United States would take in the growing conflict with Germany. On this trip down the bay, Dr. Grayson, who was familiar with the Hampton course, urged the president to take a break. President Wilson, an avid golfer who played almost daily, followed the doctor's advice and instructed the *Mayflower*, the presidential yacht, to stop at Old Point Comfort.

The *Mayflower* arrived at 11:30 a.m. on Saturday the fifteenth and anchored off Old Point Comfort. As this visit was unexpected and was to be a private stop, the president ordered that no formal advance notice be given. Even the presidential flag was not flown on the yacht. He simply wanted to enjoy the day and play a round of golf. So, with none of the fanfare that usually goes along with a presidential visit, President Wilson quietly came ashore at Old Point at 2:30 p.m. in the presidential launch.

The president's party, including Dr. Grayson and a couple secret service agents, was picked up by Hampton's Dr. Edward Blackmore and driven to the club. Only after President Wilson was on his way did word get out that he had come ashore. This news sent the personnel of the Hotel Chamberlin into a frenzy as they readied everything for a presidential visit.

President Wilson and Dr. Grayson played two rounds (eighteen holes) in just over two hours. A *Daily Press* reporter, who had received word of the visit, and a few golfers still playing when the president arrived were permitted by the Secret Service to follow the president around the course at close range, but there were strict orders not to disturb him, and no interviews were granted to the reporter. Occasionally, President Wilson stopped to view the drives and putts of the others on the course. Afterward, Dr. Grayson gave a short interview with the local reporter, and both men registered in the club's visitors' book.

Newspapers from around the United States published stories on their front pages about the unscheduled presidential stop. Some of the headlines included: "President Plays Golf in Hampton," "Wilson Stops Voyage to Use Golf Sticks," "President Lands at Old Point, Visits Its Golf Links," "Nation's Chief Executive Goes Ashore Practically Incognito for Pleasure" and "Wilson Breaks Voyage…Halts *Mayflower* at Old Point and Goes Ashore for Golf." On the way back to Old Point, the presidential party took in some of the historic sites in Hampton and made a brief stop at Fort Monroe. Around 5:30 p.m., the group left Old Point for the voyage to New York City. Reports of other visits to the golf club by President Wilson came from eyewitness accounts of Jane Veneratis, who grew up on Hampton Roads Avenue. Mrs. Veneratis was asked to do an oral history of her life in the 1980s, and when asked about the golf course, she noted:

One pleasant day, Mother and I were sitting on the porch reading when she said, "Why, that looks like President Wilson," and it was, walking down towards the golf club past our house with about two or three men. And we mostly knew—I don't think it was in the paper—but it was mostly known, when the presidential yacht, the Mayflower, *was anchored off Hampton Roads. He would come in his brightly polished launch and tie up at the end of Manteo Avenue, where there was a small but substantial wharf. And he would walk the one block from Manteo to Hampton Roads Avenue. There was no Manteo Avenue then; it was opposite where Manteo Avenue is now. He'd walk the one block to Hampton Roads Avenue and walk up several blocks to the clubhouse and play golf, and then they'd come back after a while and go on back to the Mayflower. My brother was small and he liked to investigate new things in the neighborhood, so he was very much interested in this launch. The brass was shiny and it was quite something, and the men were neatly dressed. He liked to talk to people, and he'd gotten in conversation with the men and they let him on the launch. At dinner that night my mother and father doubted that my brother had actually been on the launch, and so father questioned my brother quite closely and he could answer and describe it. My father said he was sure that the men had let him on. And President Wilson came in occasionally—it was more than just once. It wasn't in the papers; we just looked up and there's President Wilson going by, and it was interesting to see him, but we just went on reading you know. And there wasn't anyone around, no one peering at him. It was nice that he wanted to come to this golf club.*

President William Taft, an avid golfer, was the only other U.S. president who came close to playing at the club. In March 1905, it was announced that he would be attending a celebration at the Hampton Normal and Agricultural School. The Hampton Golf and Country Club was alerted to the possibility of President Taft playing there. Immediately, officials began to ensure that the course was in top form. President Taft did attend the celebration at the school but did not visit the golf course.

The beginning of the end of the Hampton Roads Golf and Country Club in Olde Wythe started in 1915. That year, the Chamberlin Hotel acquired land closer to Old Point Comfort to build its own modern eighteen-hole club. With the news of a new Chamberlin golf club, and with more residents living outside of the city, the club's demise was eminent.

In the spring of 1916, the golf club's officers put the clubhouse and an acre of land around it up for sale. They advertised that the clubhouse could be converted into a nice bungalow with views of Hampton Roads Harbor. The Hotel Chamberlin opened the Old Point Comfort Country Club in the fall of 1916. After this, the Hampton club saw declining membership and limited play, with most golfers playing on the eighteen-hole Chamberlin course instead.

In November 1919, the Hampton clubhouse was sold to the Peninsula Automobile Association Club. An agreement was made with the golf club wherein its members could continue to play on the course and use the clubhouse for a limited time.

In 1920, an agreement with the Armstrong Land Company, which, since 1904, had owned the property where the golf course was located, was up for renewal. The land company was not anxious to renew this agreement and instead wanted to divide and develop the land for residential building lots.

A devastating fire on March 7, 1920, burned the Hotel Chamberlin to the ground. Seizing this opportunity, the board of directors of the Hampton Roads Golf Club offered the owners of the Hotel Chamberlin $17,000 to

The first advertisement announcing the Peninsula Automobile Association's ownership of the clubhouse.

buy the Old Point Country Club. The offer for the clubhouse and property was accepted, and the Hampton Roads Golf and Country Club was reestablished at the new site later that month.

The clubhouse was fitted with items from the old location such as furnishings, photographs and trophies, as well as the visitors' books, including the one that had the signatures of President Wilson and Dr. Grayson. A fire in January 1926 burned the clubhouse to the ground and destroyed all of the historical mementos. After the insurance claim was paid, a larger clubhouse was rebuilt using fire-resistant construction materials of the day. From 1916 through the present day, the golf course survives. Currently, the city of Hampton owns and operates the course, now known as the Woodlands.

What happened to the original clubhouse and the grounds? The property was divided into forty building lots and put up for sale in the summer of 1920. In March 1921, the Peninsula Automobile Association Club put the clubhouse and the acre of land up for sale, and shortly thereafter, it was sold and converted into a single-family home. In the mid-1930s, the old clubhouse property was sold to a local developer, who tore down the structure and divided the land into two lots for new homes. It was rumored that the bricks from the foundation of the clubhouse were used in the construction of the new homes.

The Hampton Roads Golf and Country Club's story is one of many in our neighborhood whose impact reaches farther than we could have imagined. Without that first meeting, in 1896, of a group of visionaries who enjoyed the sport of golf and wanted to introduce it to others in the Hampton area, it would not have happened. These men had the right mix to make it happen, and it all came together here in Olde Wythe.

Chapter 10

SNIPPETS AND VIGNETTES
FROM OLDE WYTHE

THE HAMPTON ROADS DRIVING PARK

Sports played a big role in the entertainment of Wythe area residents. In 1902, D.S. Jones, a businessman from Newport News, established the Hampton Roads Driving Park, which was the first horse racing track in this area. Jones was a fan of harness racing and had a stable of horses that raced on tracks in Baltimore and Virginia. His trainer, L.K. Bryan, was given the job as manager of the driving park. The Hampton Roads Driving Park was built just south of the main trolley line. Today, that location would be the property where Saint Mary's Church and the Kecoughtan Apartments are located. This land supported not only the driving park but also the first baseball field for the town of Hampton and Elizabeth City County. The location of both parks made them easily accessible from both Newport News and Hampton.

Mr. Jones's partners in the half-mile-long track included Albert Holms of the Soldier's Home, Frank Darling and Captain Charles Hewins, whose land was used for the track. From 1905 until 1910, the track hosted trotters, pacers and runners. Mr. Jones constructed a grandstand so that visitors could look straight out and see the Hampton Roads Harbor. He also built large stables—one to hold his own dozen or so racehorses year-round and others to house horses brought in for race day. The horses had to win two out of three heats to take home the first-place prize, which was approximately fifty dollars.

Racing at the park was held during the spring and fall. During the off-season, the track was used for sporting events and picnics for local churches and other groups. Racing on the holidays was a major event in the area. Races were held on the Fourth of July, Labor Day and Thanksgiving. On average, over two thousand spectators would come out for a day of racing. During one race on Thanksgiving Day 1902, a state record was set with a time of 2:12 to 2:12.14 by a horse from Baltimore. This record stood for four years.

In 1907, with the Jamestown Exposition just underway, Baltimore businessman and horse owner Mr. George Huntington proposed that the Hampton Roads track owners lease the track to him. Mr. Huntington planned to erect electric lights to hold races at night. He wanted to take advantage of the large numbers of people coming to Newport News and Hampton to go to the exposition but who had nothing to do at night when the exposition closed for the day. For unknown reasons, the plan never materialized, but Mr. Huntington did lease a racetrack in Norfolk and held night races there during the Jamestown Exposition.

FERRY SERVICE TO NORFOLK

In early 1912, the Newport News & Old Point Railway and Electric Company started to investigate ways to increase ridership. The company had already formed the Chesapeake Ferry Company and was looking at locations for a ferry pier that would provide a faster route from the Peninsula to Norfolk than was already in service. The location selected was on land owned by the Armstrong Land Company at the end of today's Manteo Avenue. This plot of land was midway between Newport News and Hampton, the two city centers that were growing rapidly along with local area industries. The Armstrong Land Company and the owners of the trolley company agreed to form a company called the "Pier Company" to build a ferry pier in the Hampton Roads Harbor.

On October 1, 1912, the group of men signed an agreement to form the new company and set out to build the pier and ferry house and to dredge the needed approaches for a total cost not to exceeded $11,0000. The ferry

The *Annex*, part of a fleet of ferries that crossed the Hudson River from New Jersey to New York City in the 1890s. This picture shows the ferry in service prior to coming to Hampton Roads. *Courtesy of the Mariners' Museum.*

house was designed and built to have a refreshment area, a shoeshine stand and, in order to determine shipping costs, scales for weighing freight destined for Norfolk.

The early ferries around Hampton Roads were one-sided, which meant that patrons had to use the same side for both entering and exiting. The ferry had to turn around and back into the pier, which took additional time. In 1907, with increased numbers of people headed to the Jamestown Exhibition, the Hampton Roads area saw its first use of double-ended ferries brought in by the C&O Railway in Newport News when it contracted with a ferry company for the use of the ferry.

The Chesapeake Ferry Company wanted to regularly use double-ended ferries, which would be the first usage of such ferries in routine service across the harbor. In 1911, the company bought its first ferry from the Pennsylvania Railroad Company. Called the *Annex*, it was built in 1895 by the Jackson and Sharp Company of Wilmington, Delaware. The *Annex*, one of many ferries with that name, had taken passengers from Jersey City at the Pennsylvania Rail Terminal to Brooklyn, New York, by way of the Hudson River. It was taken out of service in 1910.

The Chesapeake Ferry Company launched its new ferry, renamed the *Warwick*, on February 1, 1913. It could make the crossing to Pine Beach in Norfolk in about one hour. The ferry company aligned its schedule with that of the streetcars so that passengers would not have to wait long for a trip across the harbor to Norfolk.

The *Warwick*'s first daily crossing was at 6:00 a.m., followed by another crossing at 7:00 a.m. After this, the schedule would change to a crossing every one hour and fifteen minutes until the last crossing from Hampton at 10:00 p.m. and the return crossing from Norfolk at 10:45 p.m.

One of the main reasons the *Warwick* was bought was that it could be used to carry automobiles, trucks and other wheeled vehicles across the harbor. The automobile was gaining popularity in the area, and the ferry company wanted to be sure it was ready.

On February 1, 1913, the *Daily Press* announced the new service across the harbor. A few days before this announcement, the ferry company had run its first ad announcing the new ferry and listing time schedules and rates. The ad read in part:

The large (spacious) double-decker and double-ended ferry steamer "Warwick" will be operated between Pine Beach and Hampton Roads Pier...connecting with the Newport News & Old Point Railway & Electric Company at Hampton Roads Pier for Newport News, Hampton, Phoebus, and Old Point, connecting with Virginia Railway & Power Company cars at Pine Beach for Norfolk. This splendid steamer is especially adapted to carry automobiles and all kinds of vehicles, as well as passengers...giving the public fourteen round trips between the Peninsula and Pine Beach daily.

Rates for One Way

- Passenger automobiles with driver: over two thousand pounds, $1.00; under two thousand pounds, $0.75
- Vans: large, $1.50; medium, $1.00; small, $0.75
- Double-team horse and wagon, $1.00; single-team horse and wagon, $0.75

- Motorcycle and rider, $0.50; bicycle and rider, $0.25; horse and rider $0.75
- Livestock: $0.75 each for cattle and horses including attendant; $0.20 each for hogs, sheep and lambs including attendant

Crossings went on without a hitch for the first nine months of operation. Then, on November 1, 1913, the ferry was taken out of service for repairs. This was the first of many times that the *Warwick* was taken out of service for different reasons, the main one being that the channel to the dock would fill in with sediment. When this happened, the *Warwick* would run aground, resulting in damage to the hull. If it were noticed before the ferry grounded, the company would take the ship out of service for the time necessary to re-dredge the channel. When the ferry was out of service, people and goods would have to leave the Peninsula from Old Point Comfort or from the downtown Newport News piers.

The "new" ferry pier for the *Warwick* at the small boat harbor in Newport News. *Courtesy of Greg Siegel.*

During the first year of operation, the ferry company did not see the traffic that it had hoped for when planning the new crossing. With the traffic not meeting expectations coupled with the costs of continually dredging the channel to the pier, the company started to look at other locations for a crossing. Late in 1912, Newport News built a city-owned dock that it hoped would spark economic development. Called the Small Boat Harbor, the new dock was opened at Salters Creek in 1914. The ferry company took advantage of the new dock and closed the pier at the end of Manteo Avenue. The Chesapeake Ferry Company was very successful, its ferries running until 1948, when the Virginia Department of Transportation bought the company. The VDOT continued to run the ferries across Hampton Roads until 1952, when the Hampton Roads Bridge Tunnel opened.

What about the pier at Manteo Avenue? It lasted quite a while, but storms slowly tore it apart over the years. Today, if you stand at the shoreline at low tide, you can still see a few pilings sticking out from the water.

HAMPTON ROADS GOLF AND COUNTRY CLUB TENNIS CHAMPIONSHIP

Sports continued to be part of the social life of the residents of Wythe and the surrounding area. In 1905, the Hampton Roads Golf and County Club sponsored the first tennis championship on the Peninsula, with women's and men's singles matches held at the club's courts. Players from Hampton, Old Point and Newport News participated in these matches. After that first event in 1905, tennis around the area became more popular, with more and more people taking up the sport.

By 1922, interest in tennis had become so great that the Kecoughtan Tennis Club was formed by a group of players who lived along the Boulevard. One of the members owned an empty lot on Maple Avenue near Nineteenth Street, which today is part of the city of Newport News. It was on this lot that the club built its first tennis court.

After its original site off Kecoughtan Road was sold, the club needed to come up with the funds needed to move to another site. In 1935, Captain John Robinson, along with two business partners who were plotting home lots in the area, offered a tract of three and a half acres to county supervisors for a park to be named the John C. Robinson Park, and the

First awarded in 1905 at the Hampton Roads Golf and County Club, this trophy went on to be used by the Kecatan Tennis Club until the 1930s. *Courtesy of Hampton History Museum.*

county accepted the offer. At the same meeting, Robinson also requested that the supervisors give the site to the Kecoughtan Tennis Club so it could build a clubhouse and tennis courts. The president of the club addressed the supervisors and shared how it had grown into one of the largest recreation clubs in the area. It was stated that funds for the construction of the new clubhouse and courts would come from the Works Project Administration (WPA) and that county would not have to pay.

However, the Commonwealth's Attorney informed the supervisors that public land could not be built upon if it was to be used by an organization that restricted its membership. The supervisors tabled the issue in order to further investigate the matter. Eventually, an unfavorable ruling came down, and the tennis club never came to fruition. What did result was a pubic park with playground equipment and a "park house," a six-sided, open-roofed building with a fireplace that was available for group outings. Over the years, the park house hosted scout meetings as well as school groups from the nearby Wythe School.

THE BANK OF HAMPTON ROADS

The Kecoughtan business section welcomed a new, modern bank building in 1942 when the Bank of Hampton Roads opened a branch at the intersection of Kecoughtan Road and Pocahontas Place.

The building would be unique among other banks in the area. Sitting back four hundred feet from the road, it had a landscaped courtyard in front of the main entrance. With the large lot, parking was available on both sides of the building, which prompted the architects to design a second bank entrance on the west side of the building. At the time, having two entrances was unheard of for bank buildings.

Another unique feature of the building was the drive-up transaction window called an "Auto Customer Window," the area's first. The bulletproof window was electric, allowing the teller to open it with the touch of a button. Once the small window opened, the customer would pass his or her transaction to the teller. Of all of the bank's modern features, this was by far the most talked about. The bank owner filled the newspapers with ads boasting that when you banked at the Bank of Hampton Roads, you did not have to park your car and walk into the bank. All of your banking needs could be handled at the new drive-up window.

Today, you can see the outline of these unique features. The front door is no longer used, but you can still see where it was located, and the courtyard in front still adds a little green space to all the blacktop. The original drive-up window is long gone, but if you look on the east side of the building, you will see a little protruding section that is covered with wood and painted to blend in with the building. This was where the original drive-up window was located. Even though many things have changed, when you see the building, you can still go back in time and think of what it was like to be at the branch during its grand opening in the spring of 1942.

THE JAMESTOWN CENTENNIAL

In 1907, the Jamestown Centennial opened on the grounds of what is today the naval base across the Hampton Roads Harbor within sight of Olde Wythe. The exposition was planned for years and was what we would call a world's fair, with many countries showcasing their cultures in different buildings throughout the grounds.

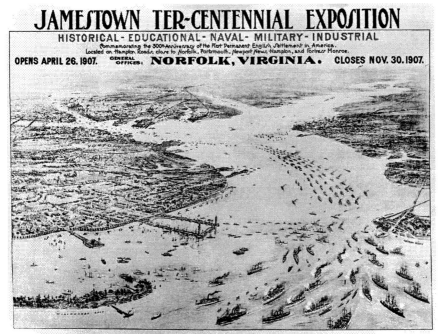

An overview of the Jamestown Centennial Exposition of 1907. *Courtesy of John Lawson.*

In 1906, a local company called the Hampton Roads Villa Company, formed in 1899 as a development agency, made plans to build a pier located between today's Claremont and Pear Avenues. The majority of the company's officers lived near or on the Boulevard and wanted to take advantage of its proximity to the exhibition. The company was hoping to profit from building a pier for passenger ships at the shortest distance from Hampton to the exhibition.

Work on the pier began in August 1906. Approximately 1,150 feet long by 20 feet wide, the pier ended in 80 feet of water so that large harbor steamers would not have to worry about running aground at low tide. Located at the end of the pier was a large pavilion, with two smaller pavilions spaced out along the length of the pier. The investors also used the sides of the pier to lease out dock space as well as personal docks for their own pleasure boats.

In the spring of 1907, the pier company ran ads in the local paper looking for steamers to rent the pier. In June of that year, the *Edna B*, a small steamer, started taking passengers from the Boulevard pier to the exhibition. Starting at 6:30 a.m., it made three round trips daily, with the last arrival from the exhibition to the Boulevard at 10:00 p.m. The *Edna B* made stops in Hampton before crossing the harbor and dropping passengers at the exhibition's grounds.

USS *MONITOR*

In 1973, a debate began after the discovery of the USS *Monitor* wreck site in waters off Cape Hatteras along the North Carolina coast. From Washington, D.C., to North Carolina, politicians and everyday citizens who had an interest in the *Monitor* started to position themselves and the areas they represented to host a museum. The local Hampton newspaper published an article in which it proposed building a USS *Monitor* Park along Chesapeake Avenue in Olde Wythe. The article quoted a local history buff who stated that the city of Hampton should buy several of the old houses, raze them and build a waterfront park to house the *Monitor*'s remains so the ship could return to the waters of Hampton Roads, where the great Battle of the Ironclads had taken place.

After numerous dives since 1972 to map out the area of the sunken ship, it wasn't until 1998 that the first artifacts, the ship's propeller and other smaller pieces, were raised from the wreck site. By that time, debates were continuing about where to restore and display the ship's remains. It was finally decided that the Mariners' Museum in Newport News was the most logical site on which to build a center to house the thousands of artifacts that had been discovered over the years. In addition to telling the story of the Battle of Hampton Roads, the museum would also house a conservation laboratory for restoring the artifacts. In 2007, the 63,500-square-foot center opened with great fanfare. The Monitor Center includes a full-scale replica of the *Monitor* among the many interactive displays, along with one of the largest state-of-the-art conservation facilities on the East Coast. Over 1,200 artifacts will be conserved at the Monitor Center.

Chapter 11

FOOTPRINTS IN THE SAND

The Olde Wythe neighborhood has witnessed and participated in many well-known historic events during the past five-hundred-plus years. Many of these events are discussed in much more detail, with related pictures, throughout this book. The following timeline identifies significant events in the history of the Wythe area.

1500s: Spanish Jesuits explore Hampton Roads and trade with the Kecoughtan Indians of Chief Powhatan's chiefdom.

April 1607: English settlers under the command of Captain Christopher Newport and aboard the *Susan Constant, Discovery* and *Godspeed* sail past Wythe shores on their way to establish the first permanent English-speaking colony at Jamestown in colonial Virginia.

July 9, 1610: Colonists under Virginia governor Sir Thomas Gates seize and settle the Kecoughtan village.

1616: The first church of Kecoughtan is constructed near Church Creek.

1620: The name for the borough of Kecoughtan is changed to Elizabeth City.

1625: Thomas Celey purchases a large tract of land, a portion of which includes the current Olde Wythe community.

A modern representation of the Jamestown settlers sailing past Wythe shores aboard the *Susan Constant, Discovery* and *Godspeed. Courtesy of the Mariners' Museum.*

1705: The town of Hampton is founded and named in honor of the Earl of Southampton.

November 1716: The head of Edward Thatch (or Teach), known as Blackbeard the pirate, was ordered by the governor of Virginia to be hung on a pole at the entrance to the Hampton River as a warning to other pirates.

1726: George Wythe is born at Chesterville Plantation, which is now part of NASA Langley. The namesake of the Olde Wythe community in Hampton, Virginia, would later become a signatory of the U.S. Declaration of Independence and teacher and mentor to Thomas Jefferson, John Marshall, Henry Clay and many other future American leaders. Wythe would die on June 8, 1806, in Richmond Virginia.

1775–81: During the American Revolution, Hampton is home to Virginia's state navy.

June 24, 1813: British forces under Admiral Warren land near Mr. Murphy's farm on Indian River Creek (near the present intersection of Chesapeake Avenue and Powhatan Parkway), engage and defeat local militia, sack and burn Hampton and then evacuated three days later. The raiding force of 2,500 Royal Marines and French prisoners of war turned mercenaries bivouacked for another five days in the vicinity of Old Point Comfort (Buckroe Beach).

1849: The Simpson Cottage, the oldest home still standing in Olde Wythe, is built at 3629 Chesapeake Avenue near La Salle Avenue. Local legend states that George Armstrong Custer watched the Battle of the Ironclads from its porch roof.

March 9–10, 1862: Wythe residents and visitors sit on their rooftops and peer through binoculars to watch the steam-powered Confederate ironclad CSS *Virginia* (formerly the USS *Merrimack*) attack and sink the wooden-hulled, sail-powered USS *Cumberland* and capture the USS *Congress*. With the overnight arrival of the U.S. Navy's first steam-powered ironclad, the USS *Monitor*, Wythe residents observe both ironclads fight to a draw on March 10 in what is referred to as the Battle of Hampton Roads or the Battle of the Ironclads.

1874: John Cutler Robinson arrives in the Wythe area from Massachusetts at age fourteen. In 1910, in the vicinity of 1610 Chesapeake Avenue, Captain John C. Robinson establishes an oyster and crab packing factory. He will later add the making of bricks, which were barged to Wythe (1914); the founding of the First National Bank of Hampton; and the incorporation of the first local telephone company to the businesses that he oversaw. He built a house at 1600 Chesapeake Avenue in 1888 for his bride, Ann Eliza Cock, as well as a second, still-standing home at 1500 Chesapeake Avenue in 1900.

1886: The Chesapeake Dry Dock and Construction Company, now the Newport News Shipbuilding and Dry Dock Company, is chartered by the Virginia General Assembly. This shipyard would provide significant employment to Wythe residents.

1887: The town of Hampton is incorporated; it was later chartered in 1920.

October 1898: The Hampton Roads Golf and Country Club opens a nine-hole golf course between Amonate Avenue (now Hampton Roads Avenue) and East Avenue. This course would close in the spring of 1920, and the land would be developed for housing.

September 1898: The La Salle Institute, a college of the Catholic Christian Brothers, opens in a three-story building on property located between La Salle Avenue and Church Creek.

1899: Property from Indian River to East Avenue and bounded on the south by Hampton Roads Harbor and north by Shell Road is purchased by the Armstrong Land and Improvement Company.

1905: The Hampton Roads Traction Company begins a new route from the East End of Newport News that crosses Salter's Creek, follows the Boulevard (now Chesapeake Avenue) east, travels north on La Salle Avenue and then takes Victoria Avenue into Hampton.

1906: Buxton Hospital opens on the corner of today's Chesapeake and Buxton Avenues. In 1953, the hospital's name was changed to Mary Immaculate Hospital. In 1980, it was remodeled and reopened as the Riverside Rehabilitation Center.

April 26–December 1, 1907: Visitors to the Jamestown Centennial Exposition, located at what is today the Norfolk Naval Base, are accommodated at local hotels, boardinghouses and private homes in Wythe. The Old Point View Hotel, located at the corner of La Salle Avenue and the Boulevard (now Chesapeake Avenue), and the nearby Bay Bank boardinghouse provided rooms, hot meals and coordinated ferry transportation to the exposition, which deported from Manteo Avenue. The exposition commemorated the 300th anniversary of the founding of Jamestown.

December 16, 1907: Residents and visitors standing on Wythe's shoreline and piers wave farewell to President Theodore Roosevelt's Great White Fleet, which included sixteen battleships and departed Hampton Roads to circumnavigate the globe. The fleet returned to Hampton Roads on February 22, 1909.

1909: The George Wythe School opens, and the Wythe Fire Company is founded.

Above: The Great White Fleet anchored off Wythe shores prior to departing Hampton Roads on December 16, 1907. *Courtesy of the Mariners' Museum.*

Left: Streetcar tracks on the Boulevard destroyed as a result of the August 1933 hurricane. *Courtesy of the Mariners' Museum.*

147

1912: A passenger ferry operates from the dock on Manteo Avenue to Norfolk until moving to deeper water at the Newport News small boat harbor in 1914.

July 27, 1913: Ivy Memorial Baptist Church is organized with twenty-six charter members and begins meeting at the home of Mr. and Mrs. Warren Smith on Chesapeake Avenue.

May 1915: President Woodrow Wilson played two rounds of golf at the Hampton Roads Golf and Country Club after arriving in Wythe by car from the Old Point dock at the Chamberlin hotel.

January 1, 1916: Kecoughtan, Virginia, with a population of 1,009, is incorporated. At the request of its residents, it was annexed to Newport News on January 1, 1927.

May 1, 1916: One of the first planned communities in the United States opens at Indian River Park.

January 1921: Wythe Presbyterian Church was founded as a Sunday school. Its members moved to its current location at the corner of Robinson and Kecoughtan Roads in 1940 and added additional space in June 1948.

1922: The Armstrong School opens at 3401 Matoaka Road.

August 23, 1933: One of the most destructive hurricanes to strike Wythe washes out the streetcar tracks along the Boulevard (now Chesapeake Avenue). The streetcars never again operated in Wythe and, after the Boulevard was repaired, were replaced by buses.

1934: Raymond Brown, best known as the inventor of the bottle opener and owner of the Newport News Coca-Cola franchise, settles at 1221 Chesapeake Avenue. His wife, Evelyn McCormick Brown, will live in the "Coca-Cola Brown" house for sixty-nine years until she passes away on August 13, 2003, at age ninety-nine.

1937: Aldersgate United Methodist opens its doors for worship on Wythe Parkway.

1937: George Wythe Junior High School opens on Claremont Avenue, and George Wythe School becomes an elementary school.

1939: The Wythe Center shopping center opens.

1941: A U.S. Army antiaircraft acoustic sound locating post, designed to identify approaching enemy aircraft by the sound of their engines, is activated at 2308 Chesapeake Avenue. After the site is closed, a Teen Club for Wythe teens is opened in a remaining army Quonset hut in November 1944.

December 7, 1941: Mr. Raymond B. Bottom, the president of the *Daily Press* and resident of 103 Powhatan Parkway, publishes a "Special Edition" with news of the Japanese attack on Pearl Harbor in Hawaii.

October 24, 1942: A total of twenty-eight cargo and transport ships carrying thirty-three thousand men of the U.S. Army's Western Task Force under the command of Major General George S. Patton Jr., with accompanying naval forces, sail from the Port of Hampton Roads en route to attack Axis forces in French North Africa as part of World War II's Operation Torch. This naval buildup began in September and was witnessed by Wythe residents, who had been cautioned by the FBI not to write about or discuss what they saw from Wythe's shores.

July 1, 1952: Elizabeth City County is consolidated with the City of Hampton.

August 20, 1957: The George Wythe Recreation Association is incorporated. On September 1, 1959, it signs a contract with the City of Hampton ($1.00 per year for one hundred years) to lease land previously occupied by the Wythe Elementary School. The association will construct tennis courts and, in the basement of the demolished school, a swimming pool. Association membership dues are $25.00 per year per family and an additional $0.25 for each entry into the pool and $0.50 for use of the tennis courts. Association board members include Hunter B. Andrews. The tennis courts and pool quickly become the social center of Wythe.

1959: Dixie Hospital relocates from the grounds of the Hampton Institute to a new facility on Victoria Boulevard. The hospital's name is changed to Hampton General Hospital. In 1988, Sentara merges with Hampton General Hospital, and the name is changed to Sentara Hampton General

Major General George S. Patton Jr. after passing Wythe shores en route to the invasion of French North Africa. *Courtesy of the Mariners' Museum.*

Hospital. In 2002, the hospital relocated once again to a new building in Hampton, and the Victoria site was given to Hampton City Schools for use as a future school.

March 6–8, 1962: The "Ash Wednesday Storm" causes extensive damage, flooding and the loss of power in Wythe.

March 1980: Over one hundred residents meet at the Aldersgate Methodist Church to form the Indian River Robinson Creek Neighborhood Association. Eventually, this group's membership swelled to over three hundred members living between the two creeks. Holding monthly meetings at Aldersgate and charging annual dues of three dollars, the group worked on quality of life issues, including Know Your Neighbor programs, beautification and crime. In 1980, the group sponsored one of the first neighborhood crime watch programs in the city. Some of the programs started by the group continue that continue today include an annual yard sale day, an Easter egg hunt and the Fall Festival. In 1993, the group decided in favor of dissolving and becoming part of the new, larger Wythe Neighborhood Association in order to bring the neighborhood together.

1993: The Wythe Neighborhood Association (WNA) is officially recognized by the City of Hampton. The group celebrated its twentieth anniversary as the Olde Wythe Neighborhood Association in 2013.

February 25, 1994: Officer Kenneth (Kenny) Wallace is shot and killed while sitting in his patrol car near the Wythe Shopping Center when four men mistake him for another officer whom they were targeting. One of Wallace's murderers was executed by lethal injection on November 9, 1999, and the remaining three were sentenced to prison. Wythe residents planted a tree and erected a memorial to Officer Wallace, both of which are located in Robinson Park.

April 1999: At the instigation of the WNA, Wythe's name is formally changed to Olde Wythe and the neighborhood association renamed the Olde Wythe Neighborhood Association (OWNA).

2001: The City of Hampton transfers responsibility for the six vehicle parking pullovers on Chesapeake Avenue and overlooking Hampton Roads to OWNA. The association closes the overlooks to vehicle entry and places park benches and pavers at five of the overlooks. It will later add historical markers in 2009.

2002: The City of Hampton forms a study group, known as the Olde Wythe Redesign Team, to examine opportunities for aesthetically improving the quality of life in Olde Wythe. As a result of its work, speed bumps are constructed on Chesapeake Avenue and old-style signposts purchased and installed.

September 18, 2003: Hurricane Isabel destroys the Chesapeake Avenue Bridge over Salter's Creek, connecting Newport News and Olde Wythe, and causes extensive property loss throughout Olde Wythe due to falling trees and significant flooding; power and telephones are out of order for up to ten days.

2004: The City of Hampton reduces the width of Chesapeake Avenue from four to two travel lanes. The foresight of this measure, in addition to the later installation of speed bumps, was immediately evident in the form of reduced traffic flow and the number of speeding vehicles. It significantly improved the quality of life of Chesapeake Avenue and Olde Wythe residents.

January 25, 2006: The Kecoughtan Corridor Master Plan, which provided a blueprint for revitalizing the homes, offices and businesses along Kecoughtan Road, is submitted to the Hampton City Council. As of the printing of this book, two phases of this plan have been completed.

September 2008: After a coordinated effort between the City of Hampton and the volunteers of the Olde Wythe Neighborhood Association, the Olde Wythe neighborhood was placed on the Virginia Landmarks Registry, to be followed by inclusion on the National Registry of Historic Places in October 2011.

September 2008: Hunter B. Andrew School opens on the former Hampton General Hospital site.

2010: After a fifty-year absence, Robinson Park once again has playgroup equipment for the children of the area. This was made possible by the OWNA, area residents and the City of Hampton Parks and Recreation Department.

BIBLIOGRAPHY

Blackburn, Joyce. *George Wythe of Williamsburg: America's Forgotten Founding Father.* New York: Harper & Row, 1975.

Boyd, Julian P., and W. Edwin Hemphill. *The Murder of George Wythe: Two Essays.* 2nd printing. Williamsburg, VA: Institute of Early American History, 1958.

Butler, Stuart. *Defending the Old Dominion: Virginia and Its Militia in the War of 1812.* Lanham, MD: University Press of America Inc., 2013.

Hallahan, John M. *The Battle of Craney Island: A Matter of Credit.* Portsmouth, VA: Saint Michael's Press, 1986.

Hemphill, W. Edwin. "George Wythe the Colonial Briton: A Biographical Study of the Pre-Revolutionary Era in Virginia." PhD diss., University of Virginia, 1937.

Holt, Wythe. "George Wythe: Early Modern Judge." *Alabama Law Review* 58 (2007): 1009–39.

Kirtland, Robert B. *George Wythe: Lawyer, Revolutionary, Judge.* New York: Garland, 1986.

Loker, Aleck. "George Wythe." In Loker's *Profiles in Colonial History*. N.p.: Solitude Press, 2008, 100–30.

The Olde Wythe Neighborhood Association. *Hampton's Olde Wythe*. Charleston, SC: Arcadia Publishing, 2006.

Quarstein, John V. *Hampton and Newport News in the Civil War: War Comes to the Peninsula*. Lynchburg, VA: H.E. Howard Inc., 1998.

Rouse, Parke, Jr., and Wilford Kale. *Hampton in the Bygone Days: 400 Years on the Virginia Peninsula*. Petersburg, VA: Dietz Press, 2009.

Thomas Dill, Alonzo. *George Wythe: Teacher of Liberty*. N.p.: Virginia Independence Bicentennial Commission, 1979.

Thornton, Rosemary. *The Homes That Sears Built: Everything You Ever Wanted to Know About Sears Catalog Homes*. Alton, IL: Gentle Beam Publications, 2004.

Tucker, George H. *Norfolk Highlights, 1584–1881*. Norfolk, VA: Norfolk Historical Society, 1972.

Weinert, Richard P., Jr., and Robert Arthur. *Defender of the Chesapeake: The Story of Fort Monroe*. Shippensburg, PA: White Mane Publishing Company, 1989.

Wheeler, Major W.R., ed. *The Road to Victory: A History of Hampton Roads Port of Embarkation in World War II*. New Haven, CT: Yale University Press, 1946.

ABOUT THE AUTHORS

G regory Siegel moved to Hampton in 2000 from the Midwest. Greg became fascinated by the rich local history of the area when his first job was managing the Wythe hardware store, where many of his customers would come in and talk about the past. He has served on the board of the Olde Wythe Neighborhood Association for thirteen years, three of which he served as president. He was an integral part of the team behind the pictorial history book *Hampton's Olde Wythe*, published in 2006. In 2009, he authored the book *Along Hampton's Waterfront* using postcard images from members of the Hampton Roads Postcard Club. In addition to his interest in Wythe and Hampton history, Greg collects SS *United States* memorabilia, antique medicine bottles and vintage gardening items.

S tuart L. Butler retired from the National Archives and Records Administration in 1999 as an assistant branch chief with the former Old Military and Civil Branch, where he specialized in early American military records. He attended Florida State University and Florida Atlantic University and holds an MA degree in American history. Since retiring from the U.S. government after thirty years of service, Mr. Butler has been researching and writing a history of Virginia during the War of 1812. His latest book is entitled *Defending the Old Dominion: Virginia and Its Militia in the War of 1812*, published by the University Press of America. Mr. Butler is a contributor to the ongoing publication *Dictionary of Virginia Biography* and is a current member of the Citizens Advisory Council for the Virginia War of 1812 Bicentennial Commission.

Rosemary Thornton has traveled to twenty-four states to give more than two hundred lectures on Sears Homes, from Bungalow Heaven in Los Angeles to the Smithsonian in Washington, D.C. She has appeared on MSNBC, PBS (*History Detectives*), A&E (*Biography*) and CBS (*Sunday Morning News*), and her book was featured in its own category on *Jeopardy*. Her work has been featured in the *Wall Street Journal*, *New York Times*, *Christian Science Monitor*, *Washington Post*, *L.A. Times*, *Dallas Morning News*, *Old House Journal*, *American Bungalow Blue Ridge Country* and about one hundred other publications. She is considered the country's number-one authority on kit homes. Twice in the last three years, the story of her unique career was picked up by the AP, and in May 2009, she was interviewed on BBC Radio. In February 2014, Rosemary was featured on NPR's *All Things Considered*. Rosemary Thornton is the author of several books, including *The Sears Homes of Illinois* (2011), *The Houses That Sears Built* (2002,) *Finding the Houses That Sears Built* (2004) and *The Ugly Woman's Guide to Internet Dating* (2009). She's the coauthor of *California's Kit Homes* (2004) and *Montgomery Ward's Mail-Order Homes* (2010).

Wythe Holt grew up in Indian River Park, one of the many neighborhoods of Olde Wythe, in the long-gone times when many lots were still unbuilt upon and there was a tiny Chinese restaurant at the Kecoughtan Road end of O'Canoe Place. He was a member of the first class to graduate from the then all-new Hampton High School. He has an undergraduate degree in political science from Amherst College and graduate law and American history degrees from the University of Virginia. He taught for thirty-nine years at the University of Alabama School of Law, where he is university research professor of law emeritus. He has published several books and articles, his most recent effort being *Battle of Big Bethel: Crucial Clash in Early Civil War Virginia* (Savas Beatie, 2013), written jointly with his colleagues at the Hampton History Museum, J. Michael Cobb, curator, and Edward B. Hicks, assistant to the curator. His manuscript "Legal History of the 1794 Whiskey Rebellion" is seeking a publisher.

Michael McHenry served six years in the U.S. Navy and twenty-seven years in the U.S. Army, twenty-two of which were spent in Europe. He twice served as a U.S. Army exchange officer to the British military, and he retired in 1995 as a colonel and the military attaché from the U.S. Embassy in London. In 2010, Mike and his wife, Anne, founded The McHenry Management Group (TMMG), a naval engineering corporation headquartered in Chesapeake, Virginia. Mike has always enjoyed history, and one of the reasons he and Anne settled in Olde Wythe is the area's rich history. In 2006, the first history of Olde Wythe was published. Mike was the committee chair of this first history and was inspired to lead the second book, which provides a greater depth to Olde Wythe's neighborhood history.

Visit us at
www.historypress.net
....
This title is also available as an e-book